Toward the Light

humor, insight and fun

Edited and Illustrated by
Richard L. Evans

Richard L. Evans
ncauthor.com

PALS, Incorporated
Morehead City, North Carolina

ISBN: 0-9677999-0-2

Library of Congress Card Number: 00-190126

C O N T E N T S

I N T R O D U C T I O N

I have been collecting quotes, poems and short articles for more than 20 years. I use them for a weekly "letter" I publish for my own enjoyment. The pages of this book contain some of my favorite writings, riddles and drawings from that letter along with a number of short stories and poems I solicited for this publication. All the illustrations were also drawn specifically for this book. The drawings that cover entire pages contain a "hidden" element that you, dear reader, are to find (if you can). The answers may be found on the last page of the book.

Humorous stories and articles are placed alongside those intended to be insightful or inspirational (from the ridiculous to the sublime). This has been done to heighten both the humor and the serious material. What is "ridiculous" and what is "sublime" is left to you. I hope the surprises make it that much more enjoyable—and that—<u>enjoyment</u>, is what this book is all about.

A note about authorship:

I have tried to properly credit the authors of all the articles and quotes found in this book, but many have come to me without the identity of the author attached. I have used the Library of Congress, my local library and the internet, but could not find every source. Articles or quotations that do not carry the name of an author are those I have failed to identify. I've taken the liberty to include some articles without prior permission because I believe them to be of such quality that they merit the widest possible audience. I hope the authors of those works will find me. Those articles that are cited as "retold by Richard L. Evans" came to me by word of mouth so I have used my own words to set them down.

R.L.E.— November, 1999

Dedicated to a true lover of books
and all that is found within them:
my very good friend,

Henry C. Boshamer

**Here are our neighborhood soccer kids. But where is
their mascot—their little dog? Can you find him hidden
in the picture? He's right there in plain sight.**

The answer can be found on page 152

CHILDREN, FAMILIES & GROWING UP

Mother Nature is truly providential. She gives us twelve years to develop love for our children before turning them into teenagers.

OUR CHANGING TIMES

If you are still living in a dream world where you think teachers in our public schools face the same challenges they did in "our day," compare these two lists developed from surveys taken 50 years apart in our American schools:

Teachers' major concerns in the 1940's:

Talking in class
Chewing gum
Making noise
Running in the hall
Cutting in line
Dress codes
Not putting paper in the
    wastebasket

Teachers' major concerns in the 1990's:

Drug abuse
Alcohol abuse
Pregnancy
Suicide
Rape
Robbery
Assault
Burglary
Arson

KEEPING A MARRIAGE BLOOMING
by Donald Culross Peattie

It was a wise man who said that it is important not to pick the right mate but to be the right mate. And contrary to many popular stories, it is not during the first year of bliss that most dangers crop up. Marriages do not, like dropped chinaware, smash as a result of that first quarrel which the newly married hope is unthinkable. Marriage is a rooted thing, a growing and flowering thing that must be tended faithfully.

Lacking the mutual effort, we are apt to find some day that our marriage, so hopefully planted, has been withering imperceptibly. Gradually, we realize that for some time the petals have lost their luster, that the perfume is gone. Daily watering with the little gracious affectionate acts we all welcome, with mutual concern for the other's contentment, with self-watchfulness here and self-forgiveness there, brings forth ever new blossoms.

YOUR CHILDREN ARE NOT YOUR CHILDREN
by Kahlil Gibran

Your children are not your children.
They are the sons and daughters of
Life's longing for itself.
They come through you but not
    from you,
And though they are with you, yet
    they belong not to you.
You may give them your love but not
    your thoughts,
For they have their own thoughts.
You may house their bodies but not
    their souls,
For their souls dwell in the house of
    tomorrow, which you cannot visit,
    not even in your dreams.
You may strive to be like them,
    but seek not to make them like
    you.
For life goes not backward nor
    tarries with yesterday.
You are the bows from which your
    children as living arrows are
    sent forth.
The archer sees the mark upon the
    path of the infinite, and He bends
    you with His might that His
    arrows might go swift and far.
Let your bending in the archer's
    hand be for gladness;
For even as He loves the arrow that
    flies, so He loves also the bow
    that is stable.

The Joys of Scouting

Dear Mom,

Our scout master told us to write to our parents in case you saw the flood on TV and worried. We are OK. Only one of our tents and two sleeping bags got washed away. Luckily, none of us drowned because we were all up on the mountain looking for Chad when it happened. Oh yes, please call Chad's mother and tell her he is OK. He can't write because of the cast. I got to ride in the search and rescue jeeps. It was neat. We never would have found him in the dark if it hadn't been for the lightning. Scoutmaster Webb got mad at Chad for going on a hike alone without telling anyone. Chad said he did tell him, but it was during the fire so he probably didn't hear him. Did you know that if you put gas on a fire, the gas can will blow up? The wet wood still didn't burn, but one of our tents did. John is going to look weird until his hair grows back.

We will be home on Saturday if Scoutmaster Webb gets the car fixed. It wasn't his fault about the wreck. The brakes worked OK when we left. Scoutmaster Webb said that a car that old you have to expect something to break down; that's probably why he can't get insurance on it. We think it's a neat car. He doesn't care if we get it dirty, and if it's hot, sometimes he lets us ride on the tailgate. It gets pretty hot with ten people in the car. He let us take turns riding in the trailer until the highway patrolman stopped and talked to us. Scoutmaster Webb is a neat guy and don't worry, he is a good driver. In fact, he is teaching Terry how to drive on the mountain roads where there isn't any traffic. All we ever see up there is logging trucks.

This morning all of the guys were diving off the rocks and swimming out in the lake. Scoutmaster Webb wouldn't let me because I can't swim and Chad was afraid he would sink because of his cast, so he let us take the canoe across the lake. It was great. You can still see some of the trees under the water from the flood. Scoutmaster Webb isn't crabby like some scoutmasters. He didn't even get mad about the life jackets. He has to spend a lot of time working on the car so we are trying not to cause him any trouble.

Guess what? We have all passed our first-aid merit badges. When Dave dove into the lake and cut his arm, we got to see how a tourniquet works. Also, Wade and I threw up. Scoutmaster Webb said it probably was just food poisoning from the leftover chicken; he said they got sick that way from the food they ate in prison. I'm so glad he got out and became our scoutmaster. He said he sure figured out to get things done better while he was doing his time.

I have to go now. We are going into town to mail our letters and buy bullets. Don't worry about anything. We are fine.

Love, Cole

PS: How long has it been since I had a tetanus shot?

FAMILY AFFECTION AND UNDERSTANDING

by Admiral Richard E. Byrd

The universe is an almost untouched reservoir of significance and value, and man need not be discouraged because he cannot fathom it. His view of life is no more than a flash in time. The details and distractions are infinite. It is only natural therefore, that we should never see the picture whole. But the universal goal—the attainment of harmony—is apparent. The very act of perceiving this goal and striving constantly toward it does much in itself to bring us closer and, therefore, becomes an end in itself. . . I realized how wrong my sense of values had been, and how I had failed to see that the simple, homely, unpretentious things of life are the most important. . . . When a man achieves a fair measure of harmony within himself and his family circle, he achieves peace; and a nation made up of such individuals and groups is a happy nation. As the harmony of a star in its course is expressed by rhythm and grace, so the harmony of a man's life-course is expressed by happiness. . .

At the end only two things really matter to a man, regardless of who he is; and they are the affection and understanding of his family. Anything and everything else he creates are insubstantial; they are ships given over to the mercy of the winds and tides of prejudice. But the family is an everlasting anchorage, a quiet harbor where a man's ships can be left to swing on the moorings of pride and loyalty.

GRANDMA'S RUM CAKE

(Editor's note: My favorite memory of my old Grandma is the pure happiness she exhibited working in her kitchen. I rescued this recipe for her famous rum cake from Grandma's files. I feel it really helps me to better understand the true source of her happiness.)

Ingredients

1 or 2 cups rum
2 large eggs
1 cup butter
1 cup dried fruit
1 tsp. sugar
2 drops lemon juice
1/2 cup nuts
1 tsp. baking powder
1/2 cup brown sugar *
1 tsp. soda

Mixing

Before you start, sample the rum to be sure it is of good quality. Wait a few seconds and check it again after the fire from the first taste has eased. A good rum will burn all the way down. Now, select a large mixing bowl and pour a level cup of rum into a measuring cup. Pour half the rum in the bowl and drink the rest, quickly. Repeat this several times.

Using an electric mixer, beat 1 cup of butter in a large fluffy bowl. Add 1 seaspoon of thugar and beat again. Sample the rum. Another bottle may be opened as necessassary.

Add 2 arge leggs, 2 cups of fried druit and beat till high. Simple the rum agin. If druit gets stuck in beaters, just pry it loose with a drewscriver. Sumple the rummm agin. Check it for tonscisticity.

Now, where were I? No, where am I? Oh, yes, nest sift 3 cups of pepper or salt (who cares which). Sampail rum. Sift 1/2 punt of lemon juice, fold in chopped butter and strain everything. But, be areful not to strain your nuts. Add 1 bubblespoon of brown thugar, or whatever color you can find. Wix mell. Simmple the tum.

Grease oven a turn pan to 350 gredees. Pour the hole mess into the oven, and ake. Go to bed.

MOTHERHOOD

by Agnes Lee

Mary, The Christ long slain, passed silently,
Following the children, joyously astir
Under the cedars and the olive-tree,
Pausing to let their laughter float to her.
Each voice an echo of a voice more dear,
She saw a little Jesus in every face.

Then came another woman gliding near
To watch the tender life that filled the place.
And Mary sought the woman's hand, and spoke:
"I know thee not, yet know thy memory tossed
With all a thousand dreams their eyes evoke
Who bring to thee a child beloved and lost.

"I, too, have rocked my Little one.
And he was fair! O fairer than the fairest sun,
And like its rays through amber spun
His sun-bright hair!
Still I can see it shine and shine."

"His ways were ever darling ways"—
And Mary smiled—
"So soft, so clinging! Glad relays
Of love were all his precious days
My Little Child!
My vanished star! My music fled!"
"Even so was mine," the woman said.

And Mary whispered: "Tell me, thou,
Of thine." And she:
"Oh, mine was rosy as a bough
Blooming with roses, sent somehow,
To bloom for me!
His balmy fingers left a thrill
Deep in my breast that warms me still."

Then she gazed down some wilder, darker hour,
And said—when Mary questioned, knowing not:
"Who art thou, mother of so sweet a flower?"—
"I am the mother of Iscariot."

**When the one man loves the one woman and the one
woman loves the one man, the very angels leave heaven
and come and sit in that house and sing for joy.**

BRAHMA

15

THE TAPE IS ROLLING

by Susan Reimer

used by permission of the author
and *The Baltimore Sun*

from her book *Motherhood is a Contact Sport*

There are things in this life that are true. Absolutely true. Children think they know these things. Men talk like they do. But only women really know.

Here, then is another glimpse inside the store of knowledge that has come to be known as True Facts. As always, I am grateful to those who have made these true facts known to me.

- Don't even look for the Scotch tape. Your children have already used it all up.

- "My mom lets me." The most common phrase uttered by a child to an adult not his parent. Almost always a lie.

- It is a common misconception that sleep-over means sleeping over at someone else's house. It does not. It means that after your child spends the night at another child's house, you have to do the sleeping part of it over sometime that next afternoon or your child will not be fit to live with.

- If you go back to bed after your children leave for school and ignore that ringing phone, it will be the school calling to tell you your child is sick and needs to come home.

- Where are all the spoons? Probably the same place all the other socks are.

- Old Russian proverb: Women do everything. Men do the rest.

- You know your child has reached adolescence when the field trip permission slips come with "My parent will not be able to chaperon" already checked off.

- Only mothers put the caps back on the markers. That's because they paid for them.

- Men don't sing in church. Women would feel bad for the organist if they didn't.

- If your child has a sore throat and you take him for a strep test, he will not have strep throat.

If you give him a couple of hard candies and send him to school, your child will have strep throat.

- Everything in your child's life should have a driver's side power lock—just like the ones on car windows and doors.
- Why is it that you can't remember where you put your car keys, but you can't forget any of those painful grade-school injustices?
- Women don't read directions. Men don't ask for them.
- "I don't have any." Most common response by a child to an adult asking about homework. Almost always a lie, and you will find that out 30 minutes before bedtime.
- No matter how much laundry you do, the outfit your daughter absolutely has to wear is not clean.
- If your husband asks you, "Where do you keep it?" it means he wants you to go get it.
- If it is possible for your child to leave something at a friend's house—hat, jacket, backpack, toys—he will.
- Speed dial was not invented so that little girls who can't remember seven digits in a row can call their friends all afternoon.
- You are aging like your mother.
- Women bond around problems. Men don't acknowledge them.
- Let your neighbor put up the basketball hoop or the play gym. Then your children might actually use them.
- When the chorus performs at the school spring concert, your kid will be in the second row, all the way on the right, and her face will be blocked the entire time.
- The only time you ever lose weight is after you finally give in and buy something that fits.
- Every kid in the neighborhood is your child's best friend when you open a box of popsicles.
- Every year brings another body part to camouflage.
- It is bad enough when your son burps in public. But when your daughter does—and responds to your horrified criticism by saying that "all the girls do"—it makes you fear for the future of civilization.
- As soon as you save enough money to redecorate that room in your house, a car or a major appliance dies.

(continued on next page)

- Why are there never any Band-Aids? You know you bought some.
- No matter how much money you make, your credit-card bill is always a shock.
- There isn't a laundry detergent made that gets baby throw-up off your good blouse.

And the truest True Fact of them all: If you allow your child to push the grocery cart for you, he will run it into your Achilles' tendon.

(Editor's note: this short article was first published in the *Baltimore Sun* where Ms. Reimer is a columnist. She has collected many of her columns in her book, *Motherhood is a Contact Sport*. If you enjoyed reading this one, you will certainly want to read more. But don't be fooled by the humorous aspects of this article. Ms. Reimer writes about serious subjects in a serious way. Her work is important and I recommend it to you. You may order her book by calling *The Baltimore Sun* at 800-829-8000, ext. 6396.)

After a hectic day, my husband came up behind me and said, "Happiness is being married to you." Not really paying attention, I muttered, "Okay, honey."
Later he asked me if I remembered what he had said, and was disappointed when I didn't"
"All right, then," I retorted, trying to get even, "What was the nicest thing I ever said to you?"
"I do." he answered without hesitation.

Two old friends met while out walking, one leading two small children. His friend asked who the children were, and the other man replied, "These are my grandchildren. The four-year-old is the doctor and the two-year-old is the lawyer."

CHILDREN LEARN WHAT THEY LIVE

Some times we adults don't seem to realize the power for good we possess for making this a better world through the treatment of kids. The world of the future will be the kind of world today's children make it. If today's children are treated well—they will treat tomorrow's world well.

I don't know who wrote the following lines, but they certainly contain words of wisdom.

If a child lives with criticism,
*   He learns to condemn.*
If a child lives with hostility,
*   He learns to fight.*
If a child lives with ridicule,
*   He learns to be shy.*
If a child lives with jealousy,
*   He learns to be envious.*
If a child lives with tolerance,
*   He learns to be patient.*
If a child lives with praise,
*   He learns to appreciate.*
If a child lives with encouragement,
*   He learns confidence.*
If a child lives with fairness,
*   He learns justice.*
If a child lives with approval,
*   He learns to like himself.*
If a child lives with both
*   acceptance and friendship,*
*   He learns to find love in the*
*   world.*

Babies are just nature's way of showing people what the world looks like at 2:00 a.m.

HOW FATHERS MATURE

This article from a Dutch magazine reflects the transition through which most children have gone or are going in their assessments of their fathers.

4 years: My Daddy can do anything.

7 years: My Dad knows a whole lot.

9 years: Dad doesn't know quite everything.

12 years: Dad just doesn't understand.

14 years: Dad is old fashioned.

21 years: That man is out of touch.

25 years: Dad's okay.

30 years: I wonder what Dad thinks about this?

35 years: I must get Dad's input first.

50 years: What would Dad have thought about that?

60 years: I wish I could talk it over with Dad once more.

A CHILD'S
TEN COMMANDMENTS
TO PARENTS

from *The Know Foundation*

1. My hands are small; please don't expect perfection whenever I make a bed, draw a picture or throw a ball. My legs are short; please slow down so that I can keep up with you.

2. My eyes have not seen the world as yours have; please let me explore more safely. Don't restrict me unnecessarily.

3. Housework will always be there. I'm only little for a short time. Please take time to explain things to me about this wonderful world, and do so willingly.

4. My feelings are tender; please be sensitive to my needs. Don't nag me all day long. You wouldn't want to be nagged for your inquisitiveness. Treat me as you would like to be treated.

5. I am a special gift from God; please treasure me as God intended you to do, holding me accountable for my actions, giving me guidelines to live by, and disciplining me in a loving manner.

6. I need your encouragement to grow. Please go easy on criticism; remember, you can criticize the things I do without criticizing me.

7. Please give me the freedom to make decisions concerning myself. Permit me to fail, so that I can learn from my mistakes. Then someday I'll be prepared to make the kinds of decisions life requires of me.

8. Please don't do things over for me. Somehow that makes me feel that my efforts didn't quite measure up to your expectations. I know it's hard, but please try not to compare me with my brother or sister.

9. Please don't be afraid to leave for the weekend together. Kids need vacations from parents, just as parents need vacations from kids. Besides, its a great way to show us kids that your marriage is very special.

10. Please take me to Sunday school and church regularly, setting a good example for me to follow.

WORK—AND OTHER HAPPY PERSUITS

Sometimes it's not good enough to do your best; you have to do what's required. WINSTON CHURCHILL

PRINCIPLES OF MANAGEMENT

1. After adding two weeks to a schedule for unexpected delays, add two more for the unexpected.
2. Once you have exhausted all possibilities and failed, there will be one solution, simple and obvious to everyone else.
3. Any system that depends on human reliability is unreliable.
4. Adding manpower to a late project makes it later.
5. You can't fall off the floor.
6. In any human enterprise, work seeks the lowest hierarchical level.
7. In a hierarchial organization, the higher the level, the greater the confusion.
8. If a subordinate asks you a pertinent question, look at him as if he had lost his senses. When he looks down, paraphrase the question back to him.
9. No executive devotes time to proving himself wrong.
10. When it is not necessary to make a decision, it is necessary not to make a decision.
11. What really matters is the name you succeed in imposing on the facts—not the facts themselves.
12. No amount of genius can overcome a preoccupation with detail.

The man who starts out with the notion that the world owes him a living generally finds that the world pays its debt in the penitentiary or the poorhouse. WILLIAM GRAHAM SUMNER

THE ESSENTIAL GUIDE TO
SAFE FAX

Q: Do I have to be married to have safe fax?

A: No. While it is not unusual for married people to fax quite often, single people safely fax complete strangers everyday.

Q: My parents say they never had fax when they were young and they were only allowed to write memos to each other until they were twenty-one. How old do you think someone should be before they can fax?

A: Faxing can be performed at any age once you learn the correct procedures, but usually, adults fax more than children or early teenagers.

Q: If I fax something to myself will I go blind?

A: Absolutely not! Just because you have somehow managed to fax yourself, you certainly won't go blind.

Q: There is a place on our street where you can go and pay to fax. Is it legal?

A: Yes, many people have no outlet for their fax needs and must pay a "professional" when their desire to fax becomes too great.

Q: Should a cover always be used when you are faxing?

A: Unless you are really sure of the one you are faxing, a cover should always be used to ensure safe faxing.

Q: What happens when I lose control of the procedure and fax prematurely?

A: Don't panic! Many people prematurely fax when they haven't done it in a long time. Just start over. The person you are faxing will usually want you to try to fax them again.

Q: I fax professionally, and on occasion I enjoy faxng on a personal basis. Can transmissions become mixed up?

A: Being bi-faxual can sometimes be confusing but as long as you use proper cover with each fax you won't transmit anything you are not supposed to.

NOAH'S ARK—A TALE FOR THESE DAYS
(adapted)

And the Lord, God said to Noah, "Very soon I'm going to make it rain for 40 days and for 40 nights and the whole earth will be covered with a Great Flood. But I will spare a few good people and every other kind of living thing. You, Noah, are to build an ark and take into it your family and two of each kind of plant and animal (both male and female) to be saved."

The Lord, God then gave Noah the specifications for the ark.

"Yes, Lord," said Noah.

And time passed.

One day the skies became dark and rain began to fall. The Lord, God looked down and saw Noah sitting on his front porch, weeping. There was no ark.

"Noah," said the Lord, God, "where is the ark I commanded you to build?"

"Lord, please forgive me," begged Noah. "I've done all that I could but there have been problems. First, I had to get a building permit for the ark. Then is seems, your plans didn't meet the local building codes—and no one seems to know what a 'cubit' is. So I had to hire an engineer to re-draw the plans. Then I had a big hassle with OSHA over whether the ark needed a fire sprinkler system. My neighbors also objected, claiming I was in violation of the town zoning ordinances. I had to get a variance from the city planning commission.

"Then a huge fight erupted in the U.S. Congress because all the representatives wanted the ark built in their own home districts.

"After that, I thought I was ready to start building, but discovered a major shortage of wood due to a ban on cutting down trees to preserve the Spotted Owl. Then the carpenters union went on strike and I had to negotiate a settlement with the National Labor Relations Board before anyone would even pick up a hammer and saw. Now I have 16 different carpenters working on the ark, but I can't find any owls.

"When I started gathering up the animals, I was sued by an animal rights group. They objected to my taking only two of each kind. They didn't give a hoot about all the people about to drown, but they wanted **all** of the animals saved.

24

"Just as I got that suit dismissed, the EPA notified me that I couldn't complete the ark without filing an environmental impact statement on your proposed Great Flood. The Army Corps of Engineers also wanted a map of the proposed flood plain. I sent them a globe.

"Now the IRS has seized all my assets claiming I'm trying to avoid paying taxes by leaving the country. I also just got a notice from the state about the need for a privilege license and something else about a 'use tax.'

"I really don't think I can finish the ark for at least another five years and at a cost overrun of at least 500%."

Just as Noah had finished speaking, the skies began to clear. The sun shown brightly once more. A rainbow arched across the sky and birds began to sing again. "You mean you're not going to destroy the earth with a Great Flood?" Noah asked, hopefully.

Then the Lord, God spoke, saying, "Oh, I shall still smite the earth— but you have given me a better idea as to how to demonstrate the wages of sin. I won't have to send a flood—I'll just send you *more government!*"

(*Editor's note: God does indeed work in mysterious ways.*)

**THE SAD SACK'S
CATECHISM**

If it moves, salute it.
If it doesn't move, pick it up.
If you can't pick it up, paint it.

When asked to describe her first day of teaching a class of first graders, the young woman explained ruefully, "It was like trying to hold 28 corks under water all at the same time."

When opportunity knocks—the
pessimist complains about the noise.

The secret of success is to start from
scratch and keep on scratching.

A STRONG MAN NEEDS
A CHALLENGE
by Prof. J.S. Blackie

Almost everything worth knowing we teach ourselves after leaving school. But the discipline of school is invaluable in teaching the important lesson of self-control. Self-denial and self-control are the necessary postulates of all moral excellence. A man who will take the world easily will never take it grandly. To lie in the lap of luxury may be the highest enjoyment of what a feeble character is capable; but a strong man must have something difficult to do. Moreover, the happiness of the human race does not consist in our being devoid of passions, but in our learning to control them.

If you expect to leave footprints in the sands of time, you'd better put on your workboots.

If you work diligently you may someday get to be the boss and only have to work half days—from seven to seven.

THE STRONGEST MAN AROUND

The local bar was so sure that its bartender was the strongest man around that they offered a standing $1,000 bet. The bartender would squeeze a lemon until all the juice ran into a glass, and hand the lemon to a patron. Anyone who could squeeze one more drop of juice out of that lemon would win the money.

Many people had tried over time but no one could do it. One day a scrawny little man came into the bar, wearing thick glasses and a polyester three-piece suit. The little man looked the bartender in the eye and said in a squeaky voice, "I'll take that bet."

After the laughter from those within hearing had died down, the bartender smiled and grabbed a lemon. He squeezed the lemon with unusual force, even for him, then handed the mangled remains of the rind to the little man.

All laughter soon ceased, then turned to total silence, as the man clenched his fist around the lemon and squeezed, not a single drop of juice, but *six more* drops of lemon juice out of the crushed lemon.

The crowd gasped, then cheered as the bartender counted out ten one-hundred dollar bills and laid them on the bar. Then the bartender asked the little man, "What do you do for a living? Are you a lumberjack, a Marine, or what?"

As he scooped up the money in one swipe, the little man replied, "I work for the IRS."

GOD GIVE US MEN
by Josiah G. Holland

God give us men!
    A time like this demands
Strong minds, great hearts, true faith,
    and ready hands,
Men whom the lust of office
    does not kill,
Men whom the spoils of office
    cannot buy;
Men who possess opinions and a will;
Men who have honor; men who
    will not lie;
Men who can stand before a
    demagogue
And damn his treacherous flatteries
    without winking;
Tall men, sun-crowned, who live
    above the fog
In public duty and in private thinking;
For while the rabble with their
    thumb-worn creeds,
Their large profession and their
    little deeds
Mingle in selfish strife, lo!
    Freedom weeps,
Wrong rules the land,
    and waiting Justice sleeps.

If you would know what the Lord God thinks of money, you have only to look at those to whom he gives it.

MAURICE BARING

THE BRIDGE BUILDER
by Will Allen Dromgoole

An old man going a lone highway,
came at the evening cold and gray,
to a chasm vast and deep and wide,
through which was flowing a sullen tide.
The old man crossed in the twilight dim,
for the sullen stream had no fear for him,
but he turned when safe on the other side,
and built a bridge to span the tide.

"Old man," cried a fellow pilgrim near,
"You are wasting strength in building here.
Your journey will end with the ending day;
you never again must pass this way.
You have crossed the chasm, deep and wide,
why build you the bridge at the even tide?

The builder lifted his old gray head . . .
"Good friend, in the path I have come," he said,
"There followeth after me today
a youth whose feet must pass this way.
This chasm that has been naught to me,
to that fair-haired youth may a pitfall be.
He too must cross in the twilight dim;
Good friend, I am building the bridge
    for him."

BE THANKFUL YOU DON'T WORK HERE!
(or, maybe you do)

(Editor's note: In case you can't think of anything else for which to be thankful at your employment, just thank your lucky stars you don't work for the outfit that put out this memo.)
To: All Personnel
Effective Date: Everyday you are employed by us.

1. *Sickness*

   We will no longer accept your doctor's statement as proof you are sick, as we believe that if you are able to go to the doctor, you are able to come to work.

2. *Leave of Absence for an Operation*

   We are no longer allowing operations, as we believe that as long as you are an employee here, you will need all of whatever you have and you should not consider having anything removed. We hired you as you are, and to have anything removed would certainly make you less than we bargained for.

3. *Accidents*

   First aid in most instances will be treated during normal breaks, however, application of splints, hemorrhage control and artificial respiration may be done at other times, work load permitting.

4. *Death (other than your own)*

   This is no excuse. There is nothing you can do for them, and there is always someone else with a lesser position that can tend to arrangements. However, if the funeral can be held in the late afternoon, we will be glad to let you off one hour early, provided that your share of the work is ahead enough to keep the job going in your absence.

5. *Death (your own)*

   This will be accepted as an excuse, but two weeks notice is required as we feel it is your duty to teach someone else your job.

6. *Dying on the job*

   It has also come to our attention that employees dying on the job are failing to fall down. This practice must stop, as it becomes impossible to distinguish between death and the natural movement of the staff. Any employee found dead in an upright position will be dropped from the payroll.

7. *Use of rest rooms*

Also, entirely too much time is being spent in the rest rooms. In the future, we will follow the practice of going in alphabetical order. For instance, those whose names begin with the letter, "A" will go from 8:00 till 8:15, "B" will go from 8:15 to 8:30 and so on. If you are unable to go at your appointed time, it will be necessary to wait until the next day when your turn comes up again.

THE ROOTS OF VIOLENCE

According to the great Indian leader and pacifist, Mahatma Gandhi, these are the seven "blunders" that cause all the violence between the peoples of the world:

Wealth without work.

Pleasure without conscience.

Knowledge without character.

Commerce without morality.

Science without humanity.

Worship without sacrifice.

Politics without principles.

THE CORPORATE STRUCTURE

from *The Good Life*

President: Leaps tall buildings in a single bound. Is more powerful than a locomotive. Is faster than a speeding bullet. Walks on water. Thinks he's God.

Executive Vice President: Leaps short buildings in a single bound. Is more powerful than a switch engine. Is about as fast as a speeding bullet. Walks on water if the sea is calm. Talks with God.

Division Manager: Leaps short buildings with a running start and favorable winds. Is almost as powerful as a switch engine. Is faster than a speeding BB. Walks on water in an indoor swimming pool. Talks with God if a special request is approved.

Plant Manager: Barely clears a Quonset hut. Loses tug-of-war with a locomotive. Can fire a speeding bullet. Swims well. Is occasionally addressed by God.

Sales Manager: Makes high marks on the wall trying to leap buildings. Is run over by a locomotive. Can sometimes handle a gun without inflicting self-injury. Dog paddles. Talks to animals.

Salesman: Runs into buildings. Recognizes locomotives two out of three times. Is not issued ammunition. Can stay afloat with a life jacket. Talks to walls.

Production Manager: Falls over doorsteps when trying to enter buildings. Says, "Look at the choo-choo." Wets himself with a water pistol. Plays in mud puddles. Mumbles to himself.

Comptroller: Lifts buildings and walks under them. Kicks locomotives off the tracks. Catches speeding bullets in his teeth and eats them. Freezes water with a single glance. He *is* God.

Sometime when you are feeling
*   important,*
Sometime when your ego is in bloom,
Sometime when you take it for
*   granted*
You're the best qualified in the room.

Sometime when you feel that
*   your going*
Would leave an unfillable hole—
Just follow these simple instructions
And see how it humbles your soul.

Take a bucket and fill it with water,
Put your hand in it up to the wrist,
Pull it out and the hole that's
*   remaining*
Is the measure of how indispensable
*   you are.*

You may splash all you please
*   when you enter,*
You can stir up the water galore;
But stop and you'll find out
*   in a minute*
That it looks quite the same
*   as before.*

The moral in this quaint example
Is—Do the best that you can,
Be proud of yourself, but remember:
There is no indispensable man!

**If it weren't for golf courses we'd
never be able to find a doctor.**

THE IRS AT GETTYSBURG

Four score and six years ago our fathers brought forth upon this nation a new tax, conceived in desperation and dedicated to the proposition that all men are fair game. Now we are engaged in a great mass of calculations, testing whether this taxpayer or any taxpayer so confused and so impoverished can long endure.

We are met on Form 1040. We have come to dedicate a large portion of our income to a final resting place with those men who here spend their lives that they may spend our money. It is altogether anguish and torture that we do this. But in a larger sense, we cannot evade, we cannot cheat, we cannot underestimate this tax. The collectors, clever and sly, who computed here have gone far beyond our poor power to add and subtract.

Our creditors will little note nor long remember what we pay here, but the Bureau of Internal Revenue can never forget what we report here.

It is not for us, the taxpayers, to question the tax which the government has thus far so nobly spent. It is rather for us to be here dedicated to the great task remaining before us—that from these vanishing dollars we take increased devotion to the few remaining; that we here highly resolve that next year will not find us in a higher income bracket; that this taxpayer, underpaid, shall figure out more deductions; and that this tax of the people, by the Congress, for the government, shall not cause solvency to perish.

**It's not whether you win or lose—but
how you place the blame.**

**They call it take-home pay because there is no other
place you can afford to go with it.**

PROBLEM SOLVING

According to a radio report, a middle school in Oregon was faced with a unique problem. A number of girls were beginning to use lipstick and would put it on in the bathroom. That was fine, but after they put on their lipstick they would press their lips to the mirror, leaving dozens of little lip prints.

Finally, the principal decided that something had to be done. She called all the girls to the bathroom and met them there with the custodian.

She explained that all these lip prints were causing a major problem for the custodian who had to clean the mirrors every day. To demonstrate how difficult it was to clean the mirrors, she asked the custodian to clean one of the mirrors.

He took out a long-handled squeegee, dipped it into the toilet and then cleaned the mirror.

Since then there have been no lip prints on the mirrors.

WITH EMPLOYEES LIKE THESE . . .

Some unambiguous quotes from actual performance evaluations:

-Since my last report, this employee has reached rock bottom and has started to dig.

- His men would follow him anywhere, but only out of morbid curiosity.

- I would not allow this employee to breed.

- This associate is really not so much of a has-been, but more of a definitely won't be.

- Works well when under constant supervision and cornered like a rat in a trap.

- When she opens her mouth, it seems that this is only to change whichever foot was previously in there.

- He would be out of his depth in a parking lot puddle.

- This young lady has delusions of adequacy.

- He sets low personal standards and then consistently fails to achieve them.

- This employee is depriving a village somewhere of an idiot.

- This employee should go far—and the sooner he starts, the better.

And, as if those weren't enough, try these from actual military performance appraisals:

- Got into the gene pool while the lifeguard wasn't watching.

- Got a full 6-pack, but lacks the plastic thingy to hold it all together.

- A gross ignoramus—144 times worse than an ordinary ignoramus.

- He's so dense, light bends around him.

- A photographic memory but with the lens cover glued on.

- One-celled organisms out-score him in IQ tests.

- Donated his body to science before he was done using it.

- Gates are down, the lights are flashing, but the train isn't coming.

- He has two brains; one is lost and the other is out looking for it.
- If brains were taxed, he'd get a rebate.
- If he were any more stupid, he'd have to be watered twice a week.
- It's hard to believe that he beat out 1,000,000 other sperm.

- One neuron short of a synapse.
- Some drink from the fountain of knowledge; he only gargled.
- Takes him 1+ hours to watch *60 Minutes*.
- Wheel is turning, but the hamster is dead.

We are confronted with insurmountable opportunities. POGO

The money required to provide adequate food, water, education, health and housing for everyone in the world has been estimated at $21 billion a year. It is a huge sum of money . . . about as much as the world spends on arms every two weeks.

If you are going to lead the band, you'll have to face the music.

THE TROUBLE WITH WELFARE

Here are samples taken from actual letters sent to a Department of Public Welfare in application for financial support. It would seem that the place to start with welfare reform might be in the English classes of our schools.

I am forwarding my marriage certificate and six children, I bore seven, one died, which was baptized on a half sheet of paper.

I am writing the Welfare Department to say that my baby was born two years old. When do I get my money?

Mrs. Jones has had no clothes for a year and has been visited regularly by the preacher.

I cannot get sick pay. I have six children. Can you tell me why?

This is my eighth child. What are you going to do about it?

I am glad to report that my husband, who is missing, is dead.

Please find out for certain if my husband is dead. The man I am living with can't eat or do anything until he knows.

I am very annoyed to find out you have branded my son illiterate. This is a lye, as I was married a week before he was born.

In answer to your letter, I have given birth to a boy weighing 10 lbs. I hope this is satisfactory.

I am forwarding my marriage certificate and three children, one of which was a mistake, as you can see.

Unless I get my husband's money pretty soon, I will be forced to lead an immortal life.

You have changed my little boy to a girl. Will this make a difference?

I have no children as yet as my husband is a truck driver and works day and night.

In accordance with your instructions I have given birth to twins in the enclosed envelope.

I want money quickly as I can get it. I have been in bed with the same doctor for two weeks and he hasn't done any good. If things don't improve, I will have to get another doctor to help him.

My husband got his project cut off two weeks ago and I haven't got any relief since.

Reader, suppose you were an idiot. And suppose you were a member of Congress. But I repeat myself.
MARK TWAIN

As a nation we are dedicated to keeping physically fit—and parking as close to the stadium as possible. BILL VAUGHN

WE REGRET THE LOSS
OF THE ELSE FAMILY

We are sorry to announce the loss of one of our community's most valuable families. Mr. and Mrs. Someone Else have moved away.

The vacancy left will be difficult to fill. The Elses have been with us for many years, and they have always done far more than their share of community service. Whenever there was a job to do or a meeting to attend, their name was on everyone's lips. "Let Someone Else do it!"

When there was money to be given to their church, Mr. and Mrs. Else were thought to be the biggest pledger. "Let Someone Else make up the difference," was often heard. And they were looked to for inspiration as well as results. "Someone Else will bring in new people."

The Elses are wonderful people, but of course they are only human, and they could only spread themselves so far and so thin. Many a night I sat up and talked with Someone and heard him wish aloud for more help. He and his wife did the best they could, but they knew it was impossible to accomplish all that was expected of them.

We have to face the fact that there were just not enough Someone Elses to go around. And now the Elses are gone. What are we going to do? Who is going to do the things Someone Else did?

Of course, there is Someone's cousin, Mr. No One Else. Since Someone Else is gone, we will have to keep a close eye on No One Else and be ready to take on the jobs when he won't. Most of the time it's going to have to be either us or No One.

ADMINISTRATIUM

The heaviest element known to science was recently discovered by Boeing physicists. The element, tentatively named Administratium, has no protons or electrons and thus has an atomic number of 0. However, it does have 1 neutron, 125 assistant neutrons, 75 vice neutrons and 111 assistant vice neutrons. This gives it an atomic mass of 312. These 312 particles are held together by a force that involves the continuous exchange of meson-like particles called morons.

Since it has no electrons, Administratium is inert. However, it can be detected chemically as it impedes every reaction it comes in contact with. According to the discoverers, a minute amount of Administratium caused one reaction to take four days to complete when it would have normally occurred in less than one second. Administratium has a normal half-life of approximately three years, at which time it does not actually decay but instead undergoes a reorganization in which assistant neutrons, vice neutrons and assistant vice neutrons exchange places. Some studies have shown that the atomic mass actually increases after each reorganization.

Research at other laboratories indicates that Administratium is known to be toxic at any level of concentration and can easily destroy any productive reaction where it is allowed to accumulate. Attempts are being made to determine how Administratium can be controlled to prevent irreversible damage, but results to date are not promising.

VICTOR HUGO
KNEW WHEN TO QUIT

After Quasimodo's death, the bishop of the Cathedral of Notre Dame sent word through the streets of Paris that a new bellringer was needed. The bishop decided that he would conduct the interviews personally and went up into the belfry to begin the screening process.

After observing while several applicants demonstrated their skills, he decided to call it a day. Just then a lone, armless man approached him and announced that he was there to apply for the bellringer's job. The bishop was incredulous. "You have no arms!" cried the bishop.

"No matter," replied the armless man. "Observe!" he announced. And with that he begain striking the bells with his face, producing a beautiful melody. The bishop watched and listened in astonishment; convinced that he had finally found a suitable replacemnt for the deceased Quasimodo.

Suddenly, while rushing forward to strike one of the bells, the armless man tripped and plunged headlong out of the belfry window and fell to his death in the street below. The bishop rushed down the stairway. A crowd had been drawn to the Cathedral by the beautiful bell music. When the bishop reached the street the people had gathered around the fallen figure. As they parted to let the bishop through, one of them asked, "who was this man?"

The bishop replied, "I don't know his name, but his face rings a bell."

The following day, despite the sadness that weighed heavily on his heart due to the unfortunate death of the armless campanologist, the bishop resumed his interviews for the bellringer of Notre Dame. The first man to approach him said, "Your excellency, I am the brother of the poor armless wretch that fell to his death from this very belfry yesterday. I pray that you will honor his life by allowing me to replace him in this duty." The bishop agreed to give the man an audition, but as the armless man's brother stooped to pick up a mallet to strike the first bell, he groaned, clutched his chest and died on the spot. Two monks, hearing the bishop's cries of grief at this second tragedy, rushed up the stairs to his side.

"What has happened!" asked the first monk, breathlessly. "Who is this man?"

"I don't know his name," sighed the distraught bishop, "but he's a dead ringer for his brother."

A woman's club announced a White Elephant party. Every guest was to bring something she could not find any use for and yet, was still too good to throw away. The party would have been a great success except that eleven of the nineteen women in attendance brought their husbands.

The trouble with the rat race is even if you win, you're still a rat.
LILY TOMLIN

Finish every day and be done with it. You have done what you could. Some blunders and absurdities no doubt crept in; forget them as soon as you can. Tomorrow is a new day.
RALPH WALDO EMERSON

CONTROL WHAT YOU CAN

You can't control the length of your life, but you can control its use.

You can't control your facial appearance, but you can control its expression.

You can't control the weather, but you can control the moral atmosphere that surrounds you.

You can't control the distance of your head above the ground, but you can control the height of the contents in your head.

You can't control the other fellow's annoying faults, but you can see to it that you do not develop similar faults.

Why worry about the things you cannot control? Get busy controlling the things that depend on YOU.

A three-year-old boy went with his father to see a new litter of kittens. On returning home, he breathlessly informed his mother, "There were two boy kittens and two girl kittens."

"How did you know that?" his mother asked.

"Daddy picked them up and looked underneath," he replied. "I think it's printed on the bottom."

An ethical man is a Christian holding four aces.

MARK TWAIN

THE SECRET OF HAPPINESS
by John Burroughs

There is a condition or circumstance that has a greater bearing upon the happiness of life than any other. What is it? . . . It is one of the simplest things in the world and within reach of all. If this secret were something I could put up at auction, what a throng of bidders I should have, and what high ones! Only the wise ones can guess what it is. Some might say it is health, or money, or friends, or this or that possession, but you may have all these things and not be happy. You may have fame and power, and not be happy. I maintain there is one thing more necessary to a happy life than any other, though health and money and friends and home are all important. That one thing is—what? The sick man will say health; the poor man, wealth; the ambitious man, power; the scholar, knowledge; the overworked man, rest.

Without the one thing I have in mind, none of these things would long help their possessors to be happy. We could not long be happy without food or drink or clothes or shelter, but we may have all these things to perfection and still want the prime condition of happiness. It is often said that a contented mind is the first condition of happiness, but what is the first condition of a contented mind? You will be disappointed when I tell you what this all-important thing is—it is so common, so near at hand, and so many people have so much of it and yet are not happy. They have too much of it, or else that kind that is not best suited to them. What is the best thing for a stream? It is to keep moving. If it stops, it stagnates. So the best thing for a man is that which keeps the currents going—the physical, the moral, and the intellectual currents. Hence the secret of happiness is—something to do; some congenial work. Take away the occupation of all men, and what a wretched world it would be!

Few persons realize how much of their happiness is dependent upon their work, upon the fact that they are kept busy and not left to feed upon themselves. Happiness comes most to persons who seek her least, and think least about it. It is not an object to be sought; it is a state to be induced. It must follow and not lead. It must overtake you, and not you overtake it. How important is health to happiness, yet the best promoter of health is *something to do*.

Blessed is the man who has some congenial work, some occupation in which he can put his heart, and which affords a complete outlet to all the forces there are in him.

My wife's final decision seldom tallies with the one immediately following it.   PAUL NEWMAN

Death and taxes are sure to get us all and one of them seems to have caught up with dear old Dad. His survivors all seem to be hoping for a big payoff, but is Dad really gone? He seems to be having an "out of coffin" experience. Can you find him hidden in plain sight?

The answer can be found on page 152

LIFE, DEATH AND OTHER TRIVIAL PURSUITS

Time is a great teacher, but unfortunately, it kills all its pupils.
HECTOR BERLIOZ

THE STATION
by Robert J. Hastings

Tucked away in our subconscious is an idyllic vision. We see ourselves on a long trip that spans the continent. We are traveling by train. Out the windows, we drink in the passing scene of cars on nearby highways, of children waving at a crossing, of cattle grazing on a distant hillside, of smoke pouring from a power plant, of row upon row of corn and wheat, of flatlands and valleys, of mountains and rolling hillsides, of city skylines and village halls.

But uppermost in our minds is the final destination. On a certain day at a certain hour, we will pull into the station. Bands will be playing and flags waving. Once we get there, so many wonderful dreams will come true, and the pieces of our lives will fit together like a completed jigsaw puzzle. How restlessly we pace the aisles, damning the minutes for loitering—waiting, waiting, waiting for the station. "When we reach the station, that will be it!" we cry.

"When I'm 18."

"When I buy a new 450 SL Mercedes-Benz."

"When I put the last kid through college."

"When I have paid off the mortgage!"

"When I get a promotion!"

"When I reach the age of retirement, I shall live happily ever after!"

Sooner or later we must realize there is no station, no one place to arrive at once and for all. The true joy of life is the trip. The station is only a dream. It constantly outdistances us.

"Relish the moment" is a good motto, especially when coupled with Psalm 118:24 "This is the day which the Lord hath made; we will rejoice and be glad in it." It isn't the burdens of today that drive men mad. It is the regrets over yesterday and the fear of tomorrow. Regret and fear are twin thieves who rob us of today.

So stop pacing the aisles and counting the miles. Instead, climb more mountains, eat more ice cream, go barefoot more often, swim more rivers, watch more sunsets, laugh more, cry less. Life must be lived as we go along. The station will come soon enough.

IN ANSWER TO YOUR PRAYER
(GOD ANSWERS HIS MAIL)
by Richard L. Evans

Dear Mr. Everyman,

This is to inform you that your most recent prayer requests have been received. We appreciate your interest in the management of the Universe. Please be advised that we propose to take the following actions based on your stated requirements:

1. In the matter of sainthood for Mr. Rush Limbaugh, we're very sorry but we have not reserved a place for a "St. Rush." To elevate Mr. Limbaugh would therefore require the demotion of one of our existing saints. While St. Bosco, St. Elmo or St. Egbert may not be household names, they nevertheless have served us long and faithfully. We cannot, therefore, fill your request on behalf of Mr. Limbaugh. Perhaps, honoring your Rush with a river or a mountain would do. Shortening the name of Mt. Rushmore might achieve your ends. May we suggest, however, that you not attempt to have a likeness of Mr. Linbaugh carved into the mountain side. We're afraid putting Rush up there with Teddy Roosevelt could pull the whole thing down.

2. We regret that your request to "send all Democrats to Hell" cannot be processed at this time. We must ask that you be a little more specific as to exactly what constitutes an honest to goodness "yellow dog Democrat." For example: we have had to move Strom Thurmond's name on and off that list several times. We also fear that sending such a large number of Democrats to Hell at this time might be very upsetting to the large number of Republicans who are already there. Please direct any future request of this nature to the agent in the basement, our Mr. B.L. Zabub.

3. We're sorry but your request for "eternal life on Earth" must be denied. We get lots of similar requests every day, but if everyone were to live forever, where would you all park?

4. We find your request for "peace and goodwill among all peoples" to be admirable (particularly when placed beside your other requests) and it is now in the pipeline. The mechanism by which your order will be filled has been in place for thousands of years now. Indeed, we have attempted on numerous occasions to inform your race of its existence—our most recent attempt having taken place a mere 2,000

years ago. Please check your records to verify our shipment. Don't hesitate to use this product.

Please call on us if we can be of any assistance with your smoking or drinking problems. By the way, we'll be seeing you soon. Have a nice day.

(signed) The Almighty

"Master," they all asked, "tell us please, is there life after death?"
The Master only laughed softly and said, "First, you must be sure that you have life *before* death."

Dear God,
So far today, I've done all right.
I haven't gossiped.
I haven't lost my temper.
I haven't been greedy, grumpy, nasty,
selfish or overindulgent.
I am thankful for that.
But in a few minutes, God,
I am going to get out of bed;
and from then on,
I'm probably going to need
a lot of help.
Amen.

You've got to dance like nobody's watching and love like it's never going to hurt.

WE BEREAVED
ARE NOT ALONE

by Helen Keller

We bereaved are not alone. We belong to the largest company in all the world—the company of those who have known suffering. When it seems that our sorrow is too great to be borne, let us think of the great family of the heavyhearted into which our grief has given us entrance, and inevitably, we will feel about us their arms, their sympathy, their understanding. Believe, when you are most unhappy, that there is something for you to do in the world. So long as you can sweeten another's pain, life is not in vain . . .

Robbed of joy, of courage, of the very desire to live, the newly bereaved frequently avoids companionship, feeling himself so limp with misery and so empty of vitality that he is illsuited for human contacts. And yet not one is so bereaved, so miserable, that he cannot find someone else to succor, someone who needs friendship, understanding, and courage more than he. The unselfish effort to bring cheer to others will be the beginning of a happier life for ourselves . . .

Often when the heart is torn with sorrow, spiritually we wander like a traveler lost in a deep wood. We grow frightened, lose all sense of direction, batter ourselves against trees and rocks in our attempt to find a path. All the while there is a path—a path of Faith—that leads straight out of the dense tangle of our difficulties into the open road we are seeking. Let us not weep for those who have gone away when their lives were at full bloom and beauty. Who are we that we should mourn them and wish them back? Life at its every stage is good, but who shall say whether those who die in the splendor of their prime are not fortunate to have known no abatement, no dulling of the flame by ash, no slow fading of life's perfect flower.

A RIDDLE

When asked this riddle, 80% of kindergarten studens got the answer, compared to only 17% of Stanford University seniors. How about you?

What is greater than God,
More evil than the Devil,
The poor have it,
The rich need it,
And if you eat it you'll die?

(the answer is at the bollom of this page)

*Directions***:**
concentrate on the four dots
in the middle of the picture
for about 30 seconds.
Close your eyes
and tilt your head back.
Keep you eyes closed . . .
you will see a circle of light.
Continue looking at the circle.

What do you see?

(Nothing: nothing is greater than God; nothing is more evil than the Devil; the poor have nothing; the rich need nothing and if you eat nothing, you'll die)

THE FORK

A woman had been diagnosed with cancer and had been given just three months to live. Her doctor told her to start making preparations to die.

She contacted her pastor and had him come to her house to discuss certain aspects of her final wishes. She told him which songs she wanted sung at the service, what scriptures she would like read, and what she wanted to be wearing. The woman also told her pastor that she wanted to be buried with her favorite Bible. Everything was in order and the pastor was preparing to leave when the woman suddenly remembered something very important to her.

"There's one more thing," she said excitedly. "What's that?" came the pastor's reply. "This is very important," the woman continued, "I want to be buried with a fork in my right hand."

The pastor stood looking at the woman not knowing quite what to say. "That shocks you, doesn't it?" the woman said.

"Well, to be honest, I'm puzzled by the request," said the pastor.

The woman explained, "In all my years of attending church socials and functions where food was involved, my favorite part was when whoever was clearing away the dishes of the main course would lean over and say, 'You can keep your fork.' It was my favorite part because I knew that something better was coming. When they told me to keep my fork, I knew that something great was about to be given to me. It wasn't Jell-O or pudding, it was cake or pie—something with substance."

"So, I just want people to see me there in that casket with a fork in my hand and I want them to wonder, 'What's with the fork?' Then I want you to tell them, 'Something better is coming so keep your fork, too.' "

The pastor's eyes welled up with tears of joy as he hugged the woman good-bye. He knew this would be one of the last times he would see her before her death. But he also knew that she had a better grasp of heaven than he did. She *knew* that something better was coming.

At the funeral, people were walking by the woman's casket and they saw the pretty dress she was wearing and her favorite Bible and the fork placed in her right hand. Over and over, the pastor heard the question, "What's with the fork?" and, over and over, he smiled. During his message, the pastor told the people of the conversation he had with the woman shortly before she died. He also told them about the fork and about what it symbolized to her.

The pastor told the people how he could not stop thinking about the fork and told them that they probably would not be able to stop thinking about it either . . . he was right.

So, the next time you reach down for your fork, let it remind you, oh so gently, that there is something better coming.

In my Father's house are many rooms; if it were not so, I would have told you. I am going there to prepare a place for you. JOHN 14:2

TIME

When as a child I laughed and wept,
Time crept;
When as a youth I dreamed and talked,
Time walked;
When I became a full grown man,
Time ran;
When older still I daily grew,
Time flew;
Soon I shall be travelin' on,
Time gone.

It has been reported that approximately one-half of all accidents occur in the home. Apparently, the rest take place in voting booths.

THE GOOSE STORY

Next fall, when you see geese heading south for the winter, flying along in a V formation; you might consider what science has discovered as to why they fly that way. As each bird flaps its wings it creates an uplift for the bird immediately following. By flying in a V formation the whole flock adds at least 71% greater flying range than if each bird flew on its own. Like the geese, people who share a common direction and sense of community can get where they are going more quickly and easily because they are traveling on the thrust of one another.

When a goose falls out of formation it suddenly feels the drag and resistance of trying to go it alone and quickly gets back into formation to take advantage of the lifting power of the bird in front. If we have as much sense as a goose we will stay in formation with those who are headed the same way as we.

When the leading goose gets tired it rotates back in the wing and another goose flies the point. It is sensible to take turns doing demanding jobs—both for people and for geese flying south. Geese honk from behind to encourage those up front to keep up their speed. What do we say when we "honk from behind?" Finally, and this is important, when a goose gets sick or is wounded by gunshot and falls out of formation, two other geese fall out with that goose and follow it down to lend help and protection. They stay with the fallen goose until it is able to fly or until it dies. Only then do they launch out on their own or join another formation to catch up with their group.

If we have the good sense of a goose, we will stand by each other in the same way.

Our lives are fed by kind words and gracious behavior. We are nourished by expressions like "excuse me," and other such simple courtesies .
. .

Rudeness, the absence of the sacrament of consideration, is but another mark that our time-is-money society is lacking in spirituality, if not also in its enjoyment of life. ED
HAYS

DESTINATIONS

High above the Atlantic Ocean a commercial airliner was flying from New York to London. One of the passengers was a business woman who sat quietly reading her Bible. Next to her was a man who, seeing her Bible, took on a wry smirk and said with a chuckle, "You don't really believe all that stuff in there, do you?"

The woman explained that her business required her to travel a lot and that she always took her Bible with her on long flights to help her relax. She finished by saying that, "Yes, of course, I do believe what I read in the Bible."

The man would not be put off and he prodded her further asking, "Well, what about the guy that was swallowed by the whale?"

"Oh, Jonah—yes, I believe that—it's in the Bible."

"Well, how do you suppose he survived all that time inside the whale?"

The woman replied, "I really don't know. I guess when I get to heaven, I'll ask him."

"But what if he isn't in heaven?" asked the man.

"Then you can ask him."

IF THIS WERE MY LAST DAY
by Anne Higginson Spicer

If this were my last day I'm almost sure
I'd spend it working in my garden. I
Would dig about my little plants, and try
To make them happy, so they would endure
Long after me. Then I would hide secure
Where my green arbor shades me
    from the sky,
And watch how bird and bee and butterfly
Came hovering to every flowery lure.
Then, as I rested, perhaps a friend or two,
Lovers of flowers would come,
    and we would walk
About my little garden paths and talk
Of peaceful times when all the world
    seemed true.
This may be my last day, for all I know;
What a temptation just to spend it so!

If you die in an elevator, be sure to press the UP button. SAM LEVENSON

56

DEATH IS NOT THE ENEMY

by Joshua Loth Liebman

I often feel that death is not the enemy of life, but its friend; for it's the knowledge that our years are limited which makes them so precious. It is the truth that time is but lent to us which makes us, at our best, look upon our years as a trust handed into our temporary keeping. We are like children privileged to spend a day in a great park, a park filled with many gardens and playgrounds and azure-tinted lakes with white boats sailing upon the tranquil waves. True, the day allotted to each one of us is not the same length, in light, in beauty. Some children of earth are privileged to spend a long and sunlit day in the garden of the earth. For others the day is shorter, cloudier, and dusk descends more quickly as in a winter's tale. But whether our life is a long summery day or a shorter wintry afternoon, we know that inevitably there are storms and squalls which overcast even the bluest heaven and there are sunlit rays which pierce the darkest autumn sky.

The day that we are privileged to spend in the great park of life is not the same for all human beings, but there is enough beauty and joy and gaiety in the hours if we will but treasure them. Then for each one of us the moment comes when the great nurse, death, takes man, the child, by the hand and quietly says, "It is time to go home. Night is coming. It is your bedtime, child of nature and sleep. Sleep well. The day is gone. Stars shine in the canopy of eternity."

It's a dog-eat-dog world, and I'm wearing Milk-Bone underwear. NORM in TV's *Cheers*

GIVE LIFE
by Richard L. Evans

We all have the power to give life. More than the physical ability to reproduce our race, we all have the power to make some-thing new—something that would not exist without the impetus only we can give it to grow and to bloom.

During my senior year in high school, a large group of us had come to a school dance. It was held in a barn-like room with a stage at one end. On the stage was the dance band and late in the evening, all of us were encouraged to join the band in singing our school song (yes, we had school songs then, and most of us knew the words, too). I stood with my friends and sang along with everyone else even though I supposed my voice to be less than adequate. But, no! At the end of the song, my friends all turned to me and told me what a wonderful singing voice I had and asked, "why I hadn't been singing with the school chorus?" I had never heard such encouragement before. I was stunned.

During my years in college, I auditioned for several singing groups and to my further surprise, was warmly invited to join all of them. I have been singing in choirs and for theatrical shows ever since. My singing has given me great pleasure over many years.

It was my friends standing with me at that school dance that first gave life to my enjoyment of singing. They cannot know to-day what a wonderful gift they gave me. But I know, and they are still in my thoughts and in my heart. They gave life to my enjoy-ment of something I didn't know existed. I might not have that enjoyment today were it not for their expressions of appreciation.

We may all do the same thing. Every one of us can give life to joy and happiness. We have many opportunities every day.

It's so easy. Look about you at the people you know or the people you meet. All of them have abilities that may be given life by a simple expression of encouragement. The trick is to look for things you find admirable in people and then to simply express that admiration.

Give life.

**Why not go out on a limb?
Isn't that where the fruit is?**

AROUND THE CORNER
by Charles Hanson Towne

Around the corner I have a friend,
In this great city that has no end;
Yet days go by, and weeks rush on,
And before I know it a year is gone,
And I never see my old friend's face,
For Life is a swift and terrible race.
He knows I like him just as well
As in the days when I rang his bell
And he rang mine.

We were younger then,
And we are busy, tired men:
Tired with playing a foolish game,
Tired with trying to make a name.
"Tomorrow," I say, "I will call on Jim,
Just to show that I'm thinking of him."
But tomorrow comes
 —and tomorrow goes,
And the distance between us grows
 and grows.

Around the corner!—yet miles away . . .
Here's a telegram, sir . . . "
     "Jim died today."

And that's what we get and deserve
 in the end:
Around the corner, a vanished friend.

The little cares that fretted me,
I lost them yesterday
Among the fields above the sea,
Among the winds at play;
Among the lowing of the herds,
The rustling of the trees,
Among the singing of the birds,
The humming of the bees.

The foolish fears of what may pass,
I cast them all away
Among the clover-scented grass,
Among the new-mown hay;
Among the hushing of the corn
Where drowsy poppies nod,
Where ill thoughts die and good are born,
Out in the fields with God.

"$50 seems like a lot of money for pulling a tooth," said the patient. "It's only about two seconds' work."

"Well," said the dentist, "if you wish, I can pull it slowly."

THE BEST OF LIFE IS ALWAYS AHEAD, ALWAYS FURTHER ON
by Sir William Mulock

I am still at work with my hand to the plow and my face to the future. The shadows of evening lengthen about me, but morning is in my heart. I have lived from the forties of one century to the thirties of the next. I have had varied fields of labor and full contact with men and things and have warmed both hands before the fire of life.

The testimony I bear is this: that the Castle of Enchantment is not yet behind me. It is before me still, and daily, I catch glimpses of its battlements and towers. The rich spoils of memory are mine. Mine, too, are the precious things of to-day—books, flowers, pictures, nature, and sport. The first of May is still an enchanted day to me. The best thing of all is friends. The best of life is always further on. Its real lure is hidden from our eyes, somewhere behind the hills of time.

No ray of sunlight is ever lost, but the green which it wakes into existence needs time to sprout, and it is not always granted to the sower to live to see the harvest. All work that is worth anything is done in faith.

ALBERT SCHWEITZER

Death is to us here, the most terrible word we know. But when we have tasted its reality, it will mean to us birth, deliverance, a new creation of ourselves. GEORGE MERRIMAN

DOUGH BOY DIES

Veteran Pillsbury spokesman Pop N. Fresh died Wednesday of a severe yeast infection. He was 71. He was buried Friday in one of the biggest funerals in years. Dozens of celebrities turned out including Famous Amos, Mrs. Butterworth, Duncan Hines, Betty Crocker, Hungry Jack, the California Raisins and the Hostess Twinkies. The grave side was piled high with flours. Longtime friend, Aunt Jemima, delivered the eulogy describing Fresh as a man who "never knew he was kneaded." Fresh rose quickly in show business, but his later life was filled with turn overs. He was not considered a smart cookie and wasted much of his dough on half-baked schemes. Still, even as a crusty old man, he was a roll model to millions. Fresh is survived by his second wife. They have two children, with one more in the oven.

SOMETHING TO THINK ABOUT

from *Pulpit Helps* using United Nation's demographic data from 9/1/95.

If we could at this very moment shrink the earth's population to a village of precisely 100 but with all the existing human ratios remaining the same, it would look like this:
There would be:

     57 Asians

     21 Europeans

     14 from North & South America

      8 Africans

70 of the 100 would be nonwhite

30 would be Christian

50% of the entire world's wealth would be in the hands of only six people—and all six would be citizens of the United States.

70 would be unable to read

50 would suffer from malnutrition

80 would live in substandard housing

6 would be gay

only one would have a university education.

When we consider our world from such an incredible compressed perspective, the need for both tolerance and understanding becomes glaringly apparent.

THINGS WE CAN LEARN FROM A DOG

Never pass up the opportunity to go for a joyride.

Allow the experience of fresh air and the wind in your face to be pure ecstasy.

When loved ones come home, always run to greet them.

When it's in your best interest, practice obedience.

Let others know when they've invaded your territory.

Run, romp and play daily.

Eat with gusto and enthusiasm.

Be loyal.

Never pretend to be something you're not.

If what you want lies buried, dig until you find it.

On hot days, drink lots of water and lay under a shady tree.

Thrive on attention and let people touch you.

When someone is having a bad day, be silent, sit close by and nuzzle them gently.

Avoid biting when a simple growl will do.

When you're happy, dance around and wag your entire body.

Take naps and stretch before rising.

No matter how often you're scolded, don't buy into the guilt thing and pout—run right back and make friends.

I ASKED GOD . . .

I asked God for strength,
  that I might achieve.
I was made weak,
  that I might learn to obey.
I asked for health,
  that I might do greater things.
I was given infirmity,
  that I might do better things.
I asked for riches,
  that I might be happy.
I was given poverty,
  that I might be wise.
I asked for power,
  that I might have the praise of
  men.
I was given weakness,
  that I might feel the need of God.
I asked for all things,
  that I might enjoy life.
I was given life,
  that I might enjoy all things.
I got nothing that I asked for—
  but everything I had hoped for.
Almost despite myself,
  my unspoken prayers were
  answered.
I am, among all men,
  most richly blessed.

MAX EHRMANN 1872 - 1945

Max Ehrmann was born in Terre Haute, Indiana. He graduated from Depauw University, and except for his graduate study of philosophy and law at Harvard University, lived most of his life in the city of his birth. He did not begin to write for a living until he was 40.

"Desiderata" (on the facing page), perhaps his most famous poem, was written in 1927 and has been widely distributed although he is rarely cited as its author. Some years ago a rumor circulated saying it was discovered in Old St. Paul's Church in Baltimore, Maryland in 1692. A nice story, but untrue.

I am grateful to Geoffrey Garrett and the editors of the Depauw Magazine *for their research and tribute to Mr. Ehrmann. The poetic prayer on page 68 has been one of my personal favorites for years. As you read it, I'm sure you will understand why.*

Max Ehrmann

DESIDERATA

by Max Ehrmann

Go placidly amid the noise and the haste, and remember what peace there may be in silence. As far as possible, without surrender, be on good terms with all persons.

Speak the truth quietly and clearly; and listen to others even to the dull and the ignorant. They too have their story.

Avoid loud and aggressive persons. They are vexatious to the spirit.

If you compare yourself with others, you may become vain or bitter, for always there will be greater and lesser persons than yourself.

Enjoy your achievements as well as your plans. Keep interested in your own career, however humble. It is a real possession in the changing fortunes of time.

Exercise caution in your business affairs, for the world is full of trickery. But let this not blind you to what virtue there is; many persons strive for high ideals, and everywhere life is full of heroism.

Be yourself. Especially do not feign affection. Neither be cynical about love; for in the face of all aridity and disenchantment, it is as perennial as the grass.

Take kindly the counsel of the years, gracefully surrendering the things of youth.

Nurture strength of spirit to shield you in sudden misfortune. But do not distress yourself with dark imaginings. Many fears are born of fatigue and loneliness.

Beyond a wholesome discipline, be gentle with yourself. You are a child of the universe no less than the trees and the stars. You have a right to be here. And whether or not it is clear to you, no doubt the universe is unfolding as it should. Therefore, be at peace with God, whatever you conceive Him to be. And whatever your labors and aspirations, in the noisy confusion of life, keep peace in your soul. With all its sham, drudgery and broken dreams, it is still a beautiful world.

Be cheerful. Strive to be happy.

A PRAYER

by Max Ehrmann

Let me do my work each day; and if the darkened hours of despair overcome me, may I not forget the strength that comforted me in the desolation of other times.

May I still remember the bright hours that found me walking over the silent hills of my childhood or dreaming on the margin of the quiet river when a light glowed within me, and I promised my early God to have courage amid the tempests of the changing years. Spare me from bitterness and from the sharp passions of unguarded moments. May I not forget that poverty and riches are of the spirit. Though the world know me not, may my thoughts and actions be such as shall keep me friendly with myself.

Lift my eyes from the earth, and let me not forget the uses of the stars. Forbid that I should judge others lest I condemn myself. Let me not follow the clamor of the world but walk calmly in my path.

Give me a few friends who will love me for what I am; and keep ever burning before my vagrant steps the kindly light of hope. And though age and infirmity overtake me, and I come not within sight of the castle of my dreams, teach me still to be thankful for life and for time's golden memories that are good and sweet; and may the evening's twilight find me gentle still.

GRIEF—SOME WISE COUNSEL

When meeting a friend for the first time after there has been a death close to him, it's appropriate to offer condolences. Keep it very brief and simple, just enough to express sorrow that it happened, and then ask a question that will allow the friend to keep his composure. It can be related to the death, but not to his feeling of loss. Ask if he plans to move, or if most of the family were able to attend the funeral, of if he plans to go away for awhile . . . If you have privacy, and if the death was recent, it's more likely that the person will want to talk of nothing else, will need to talk of nothing else. There's a Hebrew proverb about "wearing out" grief—if you bottle it up, you'll never soften it. "Give sorrow words," said Shakespeare. "The grief that does not speak whispers the o'er-fraught heart and bids it break."

BARBARA WALTERS

Not only should we be unashamed of grief, confident that its expression will not permanently hurt us, but we should also possess the wisdom to talk about our loss and through that creative conversation with friends and companions begin to reconstruct the broken fragments of our lives . . . We should not resist the sympathy and stimulation of social interaction. We should learn not to grow impatient with the slow healing process of time . . . We should anticipate these stages in our emotional convalescence; unbearable pain, poignant grief, empty days, resistance to consolation, disinterestedness in life, gradually giving way under the healing sunlight of love, friendship, social challenge, to the new weaving of a pattern of action and the acceptance of the irresistible challenge of life.

RABBI JOSHUA LIEBMAN

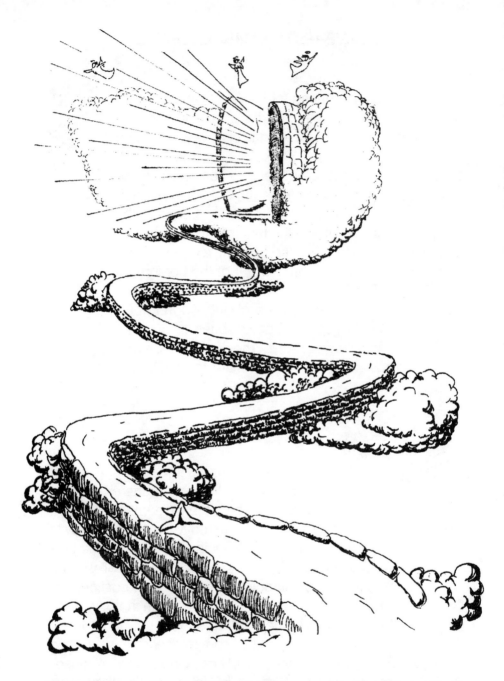

Wouldn't you know it? Just when you've finally made it to those Pearly Gates sombody drops a banana peel in your path. But if those are really the Pearly Gates, where is Saint Peter? Can you find him?

The answer can be found on page 152

"GIMMIE THAT OLD-TIME RELIGION"

My wife is a very religious cook. Everything she serves is a burnt offering.

I BELIEVE
by Helen Keller in <u>Midstream</u>

(Editor's note: Helen Keller became blind and profoundly deaf before the age of two. She did not see or hear in the way most of the rest of us "see" or "hear.")

I believe that we can live on earth according to the teachings of Jesus, and that the greatest happiness will come to the world when man obeys His commandment, "Love ye one another."

I believe that every question between man and man is a religious question, and that every social wrong is a moral wrong . . . I believe that life is given to us so we may grow in love, and I believe that God is in me as the sun is in the colour and fragrance of a flower—that Light in darkness, the Voice in my silence.

I believe that only in broken gleams has the Sun of Truth yet shown upon men. I believe that love will finally establish the Kingdom of God on earth and that the Cornerstone of that Kingdom will be Liberty, Truth, Brotherhood and Service.

I believe that no good shall be lost, and that all man has willed or hoped or dreamed of good shall exist forever.

I believe in the immortality of the soul because I have within me immortal longings. I believe that the state we enter after death is wrought of our own motives, thoughts, and deeds . . .

Without this faith there would be little meaning in my life. I should be "a mere pillar of darkness in the dark." Observers in the full enjoyment of their bodily senses pity me, but it is because they do not see the golden chamber in my life where I dwell delighted; for, dark as my path may seem to them, I carry a magic light in my heart. Faith, the spiritual strong searchlight, illumines the way, and although sinister doubts lurk in the shadow, I walk unafraid towards the Enchanted Wood where the foliage is always green, where joy abides, where nightingales nest and sing, and where life and death are one in the Presence of the Lord.

THE GOLDEN RULE

A hurried businessman plunked a dollar into the cup of a man selling flowers and quickly went on his way. Half a block down the street, he turned around and made his way back to the beggar. "I'm sorry," he said picking out a flower. "In my haste, I failed to make my purchase. You are a businessman just like me. Your merchandise is fairly priced and of good quality. I hope you won't be upset by my failure to pick up my purchase." With that he smiled and quickly went on his way.

Years later the businessman was seated at a small restaurant having his lunch when a distinguished looking, neatly dressed man approached his table and introduced himself. "I'm sure you don't remember me," he said, "and I don't even know your name, but your face I will never forget. I was a vagrant selling flowers on the street in order to make a few dollars for cheap wine. You treated me with respect and inspired me to become a truly successful businessman. I've looked for you often hoping for this chance to thank you."

It will probably not surprise you that all of the following statements are expressions of the same universal truth:

So whatever you wish that men would do to you, do so to them.
CHRISTIAN

That which is hateful to you, do not do to your fellow man.   JEWISH

One precept to be acted upon throughout one's whole life . . . Do not unto others what you would not have them do to you.
CONFUCIUS

Not one of you is a believer until he desires for his brother that which he desires for himself.   MOSLEM

Do not hurt others in ways that you yourself would find hurtful.
BUDDHA

This is the sum of duty: Do nothing to others which would cause you pain if done to you.   HINDU

Regard your neighbor's gain as your own gain, and your neighbor's loss as your own loss.   TAO

HOLY MOLEY!

(excerpts from actual church bulletins)

This afternoon there will be a meeting in the south and north ends of the church. Children will be baptized at both ends.

Tuesday at 4 PM there will be an ice cream social. All ladies giving milk come early.

Wednesday, the ladies liturgy society will meet. Mrs. Johnson will sing, "Put Me In My Little Bed" accompanied by the pastor.

This being Easter Sunday, we will ask Mrs. Johnson to come forward and lay an egg at the altar.

Thursday at 5 PM, there will be a meeting of the Little Mothers Club. All ladies wishing to be Little Mothers please meet with the pastor in his study.

The Service will close with "Little Drops of Water." One of the ladies (probably the hapless Mrs. Johnson) will start quietly and the rest of the congregation will join in.

The ladies of the church have cast off clothing of every kind and they may be seen in the church basement on Friday afternoon.

On Sunday, a special collection will be taken to defray the expense of the new carpet. All those wishing to do something on the new carpet come forward and get a piece of paper.

A bean supper will be held on Saturday evening in the church basement. Music will follow.

The rosebud on the altar this morning is to announce the birth of David Alan Belzer, the sin of Rev. and Mrs. Julius Belzer.

Tonight's sermon: What is Hell? Come early and listen to our choir practice.

Remember in prayer the many who are sick of our church and community.

Potluck supper: prayer and medication to follow.

For those of you who have children and don't know it, we have a nursery downstairs.

Don't let worry kill you—let the church help.

PRAYER IS POWER
by Alexis Carrel

Prayer is not only Worship, it is also an invisible emanation of man's worshipping spirit—the most powerful form of energy that one can generate. The influence of prayer on the human mind and body is as demonstrable as that of secreting glands. Its results can be measured in terms of increased physical buoyancy, greater intellectual vigor, moral stamina, and a deeper understanding of the realities underlying human relationships.

If you make a habit of sincere prayer, your life will be very noticeably and profoundly altered. Prayer stamps with its indelible mark our actions and demeanor. A tranquillity of bearing, a facial and bodily repose, are observed in those whose inner lives are thus enriched. Within the depths of consciousness a flame kindles, and man see himself. He discovers his selfishness, his silly pride, his fears, his greeds, his blunders. He develops a sense of moral obligation, intellectual humility. Thus begins a journey of the soul toward the realm of grace.

Prayer is a force as real as terrestrial gravity. As a physician, I have seen men, after all other therapy has failed, lifted out of disease and melancholy by the serene effort of prayer. It is the only power in the world that seems to overcome the so-called "laws of nature;" the occasions on which prayer has dramatically done this have been termed "miracles." But a constant, quieter miracle takes place hourly in the hearts of men and women who have discovered that prayer supplies them with a steady flow of sustaining power in their daily lives.

Too many people regard prayer as a formalized routine of words, a refuge for weaklings, or a childish petition for material things. We sadly undervalue prayer when we conceive it in these terms, just as we should underestimate rain by describing it as something that fills the birdbath in our garden. Properly understood, prayer is a mature activity indispensable to the fullest development of personality—the ultimate integration of man's highest faculties. Only in prayer do we achieve that complete and harmonious assembly of body, mind, and spirit which gives the frail human reed its unshakable strength.

> "Drop-kick me, Jesus, through the goal posts of life."
>
> COUNTRY SONG LYRIC

A candle loses nothing by lighting another candle.

> Lord, behold our family here assembled. We thank Thee for this place in which we dwell; for the love that unites us; for the hope with which we expect the morrow; for the health, the work, the food, and the bright skies that make our lives delightful; for our friends in all parts of the earth . . .
>
> Give us courage, gaiety, and the quiet mind. Spare to us our friends, soften to us our enemies. Bless us, if it may be, in all our innocent endeavors. If it may not, give us the strength to encounter that which is to come, that we be brave in peril, constant in tribulation, temperate in wrath, and in all changes of fortune and down to the gates of death, loyal and loving one to another. *Amen*
>
> ROBERT LOUIS STEVENSON

A man once stood before God, his heart breaking from the pain and injustice in the world.

"Dear God," he cried out, "Look at all the suffering, the anguish and distress in the world. Why don't you send help?"

God responded, "I did send help. *I sent you.*"

THE HIGHEST IN HEAVEN
retold by Richard L. Evans

Once upon a time in Heaven, the Supreme Being called together all of the great religious figures of history, both past and future. Mohammed and Abraham were there; Moses and Gandhi were there; Buddha and Vishnu were there; hundreds of others were also there. Even Jerry Falwell and Louis Farrakhan were there.

When all had been assembled, the Supreme Being stood and announced a contest to determine the highest among all the immortals. Each contestant was to use a terminal connected to the celestial computer to create a new vision of heaven on earth.

Soon fingers began to flash across keyboards as mammoth monitors showed the creations of each contestant to the heavenly hosts assembled to witness this great event. Progressions of dark and light were seen as earth and seas danced on the screens to be followed by clouds of new life forms. Sounds of thrilling music never before heard, or even dreamed of, filled the heavens. Fabulous colors spun into bursts of stars and delighted all who could see. Routines, classes, fantastic code and dialogues flew by at increasingly incredible speeds.

Suddenly, without warning, everything went dark as an unanticipated power drain crashed the celestial computer. All were momentarily plunged into nothingness. The Supreme Being touched the divine circuit breaker and power was mercifully restored. All was once again made peace and light in Heaven.

But the heavenly hosts could only gasp as they looked at the monitors. All were now blank—all, except one—that of Jesus of Nazareth.

"What can this mean?" cried the assembled hosts of Heaven.

"It's quite simple," replied the Supreme Being, "Jesus saves."

May it be, oh Lord, That I seek not so much to be consoled as to console, to be understood as to understand, to be loved as to love. Because it is in giving oneself that one receives; it is in forgetting oneself that one is found; it is in pardoning that one obtains pardon.

St. FRANCIS OF ASSISSI

SLOW ME DOWN, LORD

Slow me down, Lord! Ease the pounding of my heart by the quieting of my mind. Steady my hurried pace with a vision of the eternal reach of time. Give me, amidst the confusion of my day, the calmness of the everlasting hills. Break the tension of my nerves and muscles with the soothing music of the singing streams that live in my memory. Help me to know the magic restoring power of sleep. Teach me the art of taking minute vacations, of slowing down to look at a flower, to chat with a friend, to pat a dog, to read a few lines from a good book. Remind me each day of the fable of the hare and the tortoise, that I may know that the race is not always to the swift, that there is more to life than increasing its speed. Let me look upward into the branches of the towering oak and know that it grew because it grew slowly and well. Slow me down, Lord, and inspire me to send my roots deep into the soil of life's enduring values that I may grow toward the stars of my greater destiny.

Amen.

Going to church doesn't make you a Christian any more than going to a garage makes you an automobile.

THE CRACKED POT

A water bearer in India had two large pots, each hung on each end of a pole which he carried across his neck. One of the pots had a crack in it, and while the other pot was perfect and always delivered a full portion of water at the end of the long walk from the stream to the master's house, the cracked pot arrived only half full.

For a full two years this went on daily with the bearer delivering only one and one half pots of water to his master's house. Of course, the perfect pot was proud of its accomplishments, perfect to the end for which it was made. But the poor cracked pot was ashamed of its own imperfection and miserable that it was able to accomplish only half of what it had been made to do. After two years of what it perceived to be a bitter failure, it spoke to the water bearer one day by the stream.

"I am ashamed of myself, and I want to apologize to you."

"Why?" asked the bearer. "What are you ashamed of?"

"I have been able, for these past two years, to deliver only half my load because this crack in my side causes water to leak out all the way back to your master's house. Because of my flaws, you have to do all this work, and you don't get full value from your efforts," the pot said.

The water bearer felt sorry for the old cracked pot, and in his compassion he said, "As we return to the master's house, I want you to notice the beautiful flowers along the path."

Indeed, as they went up the hill, the old cracked pot took notice of the sun warming the beautiful flowers on the side of the path, and this cheered it some. But at the end of the trail, it still felt bad because it had leaked out half its load, and so again, it apologized to the bearer for its failure.

The bearer said to the pot, "Did you notice that there were flowers only on your side of the path, and none on the other pot's side?

That's because I have always known about your flaw, and I took advantage of it. I planted flower seeds on your side of the path, and every day while we walked back from the stream, you watered them.

For two years I have been able to pick these beautiful flowers to decorate my master's table. Without you being just the way you are, he would not have this beauty to grace his house."

Each of us has our own unique flaws. We're all cracked pots. But if we will allow it, the Lord will use our flaws to grace His Father's table.

In God's great economy, nothing goes to waste.

So as we seek ways to minister together, and as God calls you to the tasks He has appointed for you, don't be afraid of your flaws.

Acknowledge them, and allow him to take advantage of them, and you, too, can be the cause of beauty in His pathway.

Go out boldly, knowing that in our weakness we find His strength, and that "In Him every one of God's promises is a 'Yes.' "

IT ALL BEGAN
IN THE GARDEN

One evening in the Garden of Eden God and Adam were talking.

"How do you like Eve, who I created to be your companion?" asked God.

"She's all right, I suppose," replied Adam. "But why did you make her so different from me?"

"So you would like her," answered God.

"But why did you make her all smooth and curvy?" asked Adam.

"So you would like her."

But why did you give her a sweet disposition and a musical voice?"

"So you would like her."

"But why did you make her so dumb?"

"So she would like you."

THE PEARLY GATES STORY

A man died and found himself confronted by Saint Peter at the Pearly Gates.

"This is how it works," said St. Peter, "you must have 100 points to make it through these Pearly Gates into Heaven. You tell me all the good things you've done in life, and I will assign you a certain number of points for each thing, depending on how good it was. When you reach 100 points, you get in."

"Okay," the man said, "I was married to the same woman for 50 years and never cheated on her, not even in my heart."

"That's wonderful," said St. Peter, "that's worth three points."

"Only three points?" the man was aghast. "Well, I attended church all my life and supported its ministry with my full 10% tithe and I served as a deacon and was chairman of the fund-raising committee to build a new sanctuary."

"Terrific!" said St. Peter, "that's certainly worth a point."

"Only *one* point?" the man couldn't believe his ears. "How about this? I started a soup kitchen in my city and worked in a shelter for homeless people and helped build a clinic for veterans."

"Fantastic, that's good for two more points," said St. Peter.

"TWO POINTS!!" the man cried, "At this rate the only way I can ever get into Heaven is by the grace of God."

"BINGO!" cried St. Peter, "come on in!"

"Take what you want," said God,
"take it and pay for it."
SPANISH PROVERB

You don't want no pie in the sky when you die.
You want something here on the ground while you're still around.
MUHAMMAD ALI

If mere faith alone can move mountains, imagine what hard work can do.

THE FABLE OF THE NUN'S "TALE"

A preacher wanted to raise some extra money for his church. One of his less religious parishioners told him of the money that could be made in racing horses. So the preacher decided to buy a horse and enter it in the races. At the local stock auction, the horses were so expensive the preacher could only afford a donkey, but he bought one anyway. The preacher figured that since he had it he might as well go ahead and enter his donkey in the races. To everyone's surprise, the donkey came in third. The next day the local newspaper ran the headline:

PREACHER'S ASS SHOWS

The preacher was so pleased with his donkey he entered it in the races again. This time it won! The paper headlined:

PREACHER'S ASS

OUT IN FRONT

When the bishop saw the paper, he called the preacher in and told him not to enter his donkey in any more races. The next day's headline read:

BISHOP SCRATCHES PREACHER'S ASS

This was too much for the bishop, so he ordered the preacher to get rid of the animal. The preacher found a good home for it with a nun in a nearby convent. The next headline read:

NUN HAS BEST ASS IN TOWN

The bishop fainted. When he came to, he informed the nun that she would have to dispose of the donkey. She found a farmer willing to buy him for $10. The paper then headlined:

NUN PEDDLES ASS

FOR TEN BUCKS

They buried the bishop the next day.

Moral: Never rely on a newspaper to cover your ass.

IS THERE A MERCIFUL GOD?
by Thomas Merton

It is only the infinite mercy and love of God that has prevented us from tearing ourselves to pieces and destroying His entire creation long ago. People seem to think that it is in some way proof that no merciful God exists, if we have so many wars. On the contrary, consider how in spite of centuries of sin and greed and lust and cruelty and hatred and avarice and oppression and injustice, spawned and bred by the free wills of men, the human race can still recover, each time, and can still produce men and women who overcome evil with good, hatred with love, greed with charity, lust and cruelty with sanctity. How could all this be possible without His grace upon us? . . .

There is not a flower that opens, not a seed that falls into the ground, and not an ear of wheat that nods on the end of its stalk in the wind that does not preach and proclaim the greatness and the mercy of God to the whole world. There is not an act of kindness or generosity, not an act of sacrifice done, or a word of peace and gentleness spoken, not a child's prayer uttered, that does not sing hymns to God before His throne and in the eyes of men and before their faces.

How does it happen that in the thousands of generations of murderers since Cain, our dark bloodthirsty ancestor, that some of us can still be saints? The quietness and hiddenness and placidity of the truly good people in the world all proclaim the glory of God.

All creatures, every graceful movement, every ordered act of the human will, all are sent to us as prophets from God. But because of our stubbornness, they come to us only to blind us further.

My preacher's eyes I've never seen
Though the light in them may shine;
For when he prays, he closes his,
And when he preaches, mine.

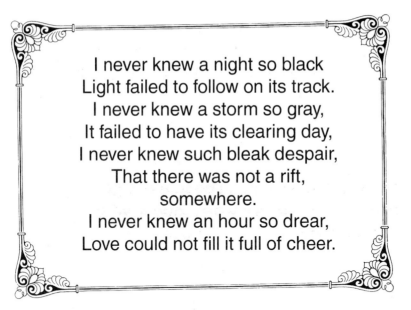

I never knew a night so black
Light failed to follow on its track.
I never knew a storm so gray,
It failed to have its clearing day,
I never knew such bleak despair,
That there was not a rift,
somewhere.
I never knew an hour so drear,
Love could not fill it full of cheer.

If you look like your driver's license photo—you're too sick to drive.

I took violin lessons from age 6 to 14, but had no luck with my teachers, for whom music did not transcend mechanical practicing. I really began to learn only after I had fallen in love with Mozart's sonatas. The attempt to reproduce their singular grace compelled me to improve my technique. I believe, on the whole, that love is a better teacher than sense of duty. ALBERT EINSTEIN

There are three stages in a man's life:
1. He believes in Santa Claus.
2. He doesn't believe in Santa Claus.
3. He is Santa Claus.

Say what you will about the Ten Commandments, you must always come back to the pleasant fact that there are only ten of them. MENCKEN

It is amazing how much people can get done if they do not worry about who gets the credit. SANDRA SWINNEY

A patient coming out of the anesthesia after surgery asked, "Why are the blinds drawn, doctor?"
The doctor replied, "There's a fire across the street and we didn't want you to think the operation had failed."

You are writing a gospel,
A chapter each day,
By deeds that you do,
By words that you say.
Men read what you write,
Whether faithless or true,
Say, what is the gospel
according to you?

THE ANGEL AT THE TOP OF THE TREE
retold by Richard L. Evans

Have you ever wondered why there is almost always an angel at the top of the Christmas tree?

Well, it seems it all started one afternoon on a Christmas Eve many years ago. Santa Claus was seated in his living room with the absolute worst headache one could possibly imagine. His head was throbbing and pulsating. Mrs. Claus was over in a corner of the room ironing the pants to his suit so they would be ready for the big night. Even though the effort only brought him pain, Santa could see the elves through the window. They were out in the yard throwing the presents in the sleigh and breaking many of them in the process. They had also managed to get the reindeers' harness and reins in a tangled mess. Two of the reindeer were even hitched up backward—facing the sleigh. But his head hurt him so much he couldn't say a word. Just then, the telephone in the kitchen rang and Mrs. Claus went to answer it. Someone with a heavy accent was trying to get the Clauses to switch back their phone service to AT&T. Mrs. Claus came back in the room a few minutes later with a bowl of hot, steaming soup she thought might help Santa's headache. Just as she was about to hand it to Santa, she smelled Santa's pants burning under the iron she had left on top them. She screamed in Santa's ear and dumped the bowl of boiling soup right in his pantless lap, and ran to the ironing board to discover she had burned a hole completely through Santa's pants.

Meanwhile, Santa jumped up out of his chair suffering further from both the scream in the ear of his pain-wracked head and the scalded flesh in an area best not mentioned here. As he hopped around the room in agonizing pain, he stubbed his toe and fell head-first to the floor, breaking his nose.

Just then there was a knock at the door and Santa, limping and bleeding and doubled over in pain went to the door and yanked it open. There on the door sill stood a little angel with a Christmas tree slung over her tiny shoulder. She looked up at Santa and demanded, "Okay, 'Mr. Ho, Ho, Ho,' what do you want me to do with this tree?

And that, children, is how the angel came to sit on the top of the tree.

Adam and Eve and the apple—where all the trouble started. But where is that tempter, the serpent? Can you find it hidden in plain sight?

The answer can be found on page 152

MAN VERSUS WOMAN — LET'S GET READY TO RUMMMMBBBBLLLLLLE!

My wife and I were happy for twenty years. Then we met.
RODNEY DANGERFIELD

MEN

Men are what women marry.

They have two hands, two feet, and sometimes two wives—but never more than one dollar or more than one idea at a time. Like Turkish cigarettes, they are all made of the same material; the only difference is some are better disguised than others.

Generally speaking, they may be divided into three classes: bachelors, husbands and widowers. A bachelor is a negligible mass of obstinacy entirely surrounded by suspicion. Husbands are of three types: prizes, surprises and consolation prizes. Making a husband out of a man is one of the highest forms of plastic art known to civilization. It requires science, sculpture, common sense, faith, hope and charity. Mostly, charity.

It is a psychological marvel that a small, tender, soft, violet-scented thing should enjoy kissing a big, awkward, stubby chinned, tobacco and bay rum scented thing like a man.

If you flatter a man, you frighten him to death. If you don't, you bore him to death. If you permit him to make love to you, he gets tired of you in the end—and, if you don't, he gets tired of you in the beginning.

If you wear bright colors, rouge and a tight-fitting outfit, he hesitates to take you out. But, if you wear a little basic black dress, he takes you out and then spends the rest of the evening staring at a woman in bright colors, rouge and a tight-fitting outfit.

If you are the clinging vine type, he doubts whether you have a brain. If you are a modern, educated, intelligent woman, he doubts whether you have a heart. If you are silly, he longs for a bright mate. If you are brilliant and intellectual, he longs for a playmate.

Man is just a worm in the dust. He comes along, wriggles around for a while, and finally some chick gets him.

MISS BESSIE GOES FISHING

One morning when Spring was in her teens—
    A morn to a poet's wishing,
All tinted in delicate pinks and greens—
    Miss Bessie and I went fishing.

I in my rough and easy clothes,
    With my face at the sun-tan's mercy;
She with her hat tipped down to her nose,
    And her nose tipped—*vice versa.*

I with my rod, my reel, and my hooks,
    And a hamper for lunching recesses;
She with the bait of her comely looks,
    And the seine of her golden tresses.

So we sat us down on the sunny dike,
    Where the white pond-lilies teeter,
And I went to fishing like quaint old Ike,
    And she like Simon Peter.

All the noon I lay in the light of her eyes,
    And dreamily watched and waited.
But the fish were cunning and would not rise,
    And the baiter alone was baited.

And when the time of departure came,
    My bag hung flat as a flounder;
But Bessie had neatly hooked her game—
    A hundred-and-fifty-pounder.

My wife and I have equal rights,
And neither runs the show.
So, when I tell her what to do,
She tells me where to go.

Creation of woman from the rib of a man;
She was not made of his head to top him;
Nor out of his feet to be trampled upon by him;
But out of his side to be equal with him;
Under his arm, to be protected;
And near his heart to be beloved.

It isn't always the coldest girl that gets the fur coat.

If it weren't for marriage, people would have
to go through life without knowing they had
any faults.

Marriage is the only place where it's
possible to skate on thin ice and then
still find yourself in hot water.

SEX—IT'S NOT HOW LONG IT IS
as retold by Richard L. Evans

After God had created the world, He summoned all His creatures to Him. First He called for Man to come forward and he bestowed upon Man a normal sex life to last 20 years.

"20 years!" gasped Man, who then beseeched God, "Can't I have more than 20 years out of my three-score-and ten for a normal sex life?" But God was adamant and refused to grant Man any more diddlin' time.

Then God called the Great Monkey forward and granted him 20 years of sex life.

"But God," said the Great Monkey, "I don't need 20 years of sex in my life—I only need 10 years to swing."

Hearing this, Man jumped up and pleaded with God to give him the Monkey's other 10 years. And God agreed. So Man was given an additional 10 years of sex life.

God then called the Mighty Lion and bade him to come forward. When the Lion had come forth, God gave him 20 years of sex life. But the Lion begged God's indulgence saying, "But Great God, I too, need only 10 years to take pride in my sex life."

Again, Man was immediately on his feet asking God for the other 10 years of sex not wanted by the Mighty Lion. And, again, God agreed.

God then summoned His Humble Servant the Donkey and granted him 20 years of sex life. The Donkey trotted forward meekly and said that he, like the other animals, would need only 10 years of sex because that was all the bucking he thought he could stand.

Sure enough, Man was once again on his feet begging for the Donkey's other 10 years of sex life. And, slowly and with a great sigh of resignation, God agreed.

And so it has been from that day to this, that Man has 20 years of normal sex, 10 years of monkeying around, 10 years of lion about it and 10 years of making a jackass of himself—although, not necessarily in that order.

A man in the house is worth two in the street.
MAE WEST

90

FOR MEN ONLY: HOW TO BE A GOOD LOVER

Once in a while, quietly, take the garbage out . . . Admit your mother's cooking always gave you heartburn . . . Tell her you never believed it could be like this . . . Assure her the models and actresses you meet are shallow, cold and much too skinny . . . Bring her one rose, from time to time on no special occasion . . . Nibble her ear while she's scrambling eggs . . . Carry her across the room (or the threshold) if you're both in shape . . . Get jealous the day the repairman is coming . . . Hold her hand in church . . . Tell her she doesn't need any makeup . . . Buy her a bikini. Decide her mother is really a sweet woman at heart. Buy her a bikini, too.

. . . Get romantic in the middle of the afternoon . . . Write her a love letter like the ones you wrote her when you first met . . Put the bigger half of the egg roll on her plate . . . Tell her you love her while she's diapering the baby . . . Send her a schmaltzy card on Columbus Day . . . Call her baby, cherie, cara mia, pussycat, lambchop . . . Tell her you need her . . . Whistle at her when she's working in the garden . . . Say they take after their mother when anybody tells you the children are beautiful . . . Dance barefoot with her in the kitchen, even if there's no music . . . Meet her for an intimate lunch date. . . Growl when she calls you a tiger . . . Tell her that her hair smells like lilacs . . . Massage her feet.

Want Ad: Wanted a good woman who can keep house, iron and do laundry, chop wood, sew, haul water, clean and cook fish, dig worms and who owns a boat with motor. Send photo of boat and motor.

A VERY SPECIAL REWARD

A married couple was in a terrible auto accident where the woman's face was severely burned. The doctors told her husband that they couldn't graft new skin on his wife's face because her own unburned skin was not suitable—she was too thin. The husband immediately offered to donate some of his skin.

However, the only skin on his body that was thought to be suitable would have to come from his buttocks. Both the husband and the wife agreed that they would tell no one about where the wife's new skin came from, and requested that the doctors also honor their secret. After all, this was a very delicate matter.

After the surgery was completed, everyone was astounded at the wife's new beauty. She looked more beautiful than ever before. All her friends just went on and on about her youthful beauty—her skin was so smooth and so pink!

Alone with her husband one day, she was overcome with emotion at his sacrifice. She said, "Dear, I just want to thank you for everything you did for me. There is no way that I could ever repay you."

"My darling," the husband replied, "think nothing of it. I get all the thanks I could ever hope for every time I see your mother kiss you on the cheek."

Assume nothing. Inside every dumb blond there may be a very smart brunette. ANN LANDERS

WHAT MEN REALLY MEAN

What he says:

I don't care what color you paint the kitchen.

What he really means:

As long as it's not blue, green, pink, yellow, lavender, gray, mauve, black, turquoise or any other color besides white.

What he says:

Can I help you with dinner?

What he really means:

Why isn't it already on the table?

What he says:

Uh huh; Sure, honey; Yes, dear.

What he really means:

Absolutely nothing.

What he says:

Good idea.

What he really means:

It'll never work and I'll spend the rest of the day gloating.

What he says:

It would take too long to explain.

What he really means:

I have no idea how it works.

What he says:

I'm getting a lot more exercise these days.

What he really means:

The batteries in the remote control are dead.

What he says:

You cook just like my mother.

What he really means:

She used the smoke detector as a meal timer, too.

What he says:

Take a break, honey; you're working too hard.

What he really means:

I can't hear the game over the vacuum.

What he says:

Honey, we don't need material things to prove our love.

What he really means:

I forgot our anniversary again.

What he says:

Will you marry me?

What he really means:

Both my roommates have moved out, I can't find the washer, and there is no more peanut butter.

What he says:

You look terrific!

What he really means:

Oh, God, please don't try on one more outfit. I'm starving.

What he says:

I'm not lost. I know exactly where we are.

What he really means:

No one will ever see us alive again.

Three successive notices from the classified column of a small Connecticut weekly paper tell their own story:

March 22nd.:
   For sale. Slightly used farm
   wench in good condition.
   Very handy. Phone 366-R-2
   A. Cartright.

      March 29th.:
         Correction. Due to an unfortunate error,
         Mr. Cartright's ad last week was not
         clear. He has an excellent winch for sale.
         We trust this will put an end to jokesters
         who have called Mr. Cartright and
         greatly bothered his housekeeper,
         Mrs. Hargreaves, who loves with him.

            April 5th.:
               Notice! My W-I-N-C-H is not for sale.
               I put a sledge hammer to it. Don't bother
               calling 366-R-2. I had the phone taken
               out. I am NOT carrying on with Mrs.
               Hargreaves. She merely L-I-V-E-S here.
               A. Cartright.

I belong to Bridegrooms Anonymous. Whenever I feel like getting married, they send over a lady in a housecoat and hair curlers to burn my toast for me. DICK MARTIN

The custom that allows the father of the bride to walk down the aisle has been kept through the ages so the creditors will all know who to chase.

A LOVE POTION FOR HUSBANDS AND WIVES
by Richard L. Evans

Like most good recipes this one has stood the test of time. Over the years its been mixed and been given in a variety of strengths, but it always works. Try it; you'll like it.

Ingredients:

a pinch of passion	two encircling arms
a hat full of consideration	three little words
a loving cup of fidelity	a spoonful of faith
a dash of daring	a bit of mystery
a grain of salt	two warm feet
a deaf ear	a tablespoon of tears
a blind eye	a lot of laughter

Mixing:

First mix the tears and the laughter so that they are sometimes hard to distinguish one from the other. Then place all of the consideration and the fidelity together adding most of the passion and then pour on the faith. The rest of the passion should be sprinkled about so that when it surfaces it comes as a surprise. Place the three little words on top so that they can be used often, even without obvious provocation. Use the mystery and the daring sparingly and with care. Save the warm feet, blind eye and deaf ear as side dishes so they are always handy when needed. The grain of salt may be taken with the potion whenever necessary.

Dosage:

Take the potion with your spouse, being careful to use the encircling arms. It may be given as frequently as desired and should be refilled often (the more often, the better).

THE IDEAL HUSBAND
TO HIS WIFE

We've lived for thirty years, dear wife,
    And walked together side by side,
And you today are just as dear
    As when you were my bride.
I've tried to make life glad for you,
    One long, sweet honeymoon of joy,
A dream of marital content,
    Without the least alloy.
I've smoothed all boulders on our path,
    That we in peace might toil along,
But always hastening to admit
    That I was right,
        and you were wrong.

No mad diversity of creed
    Has ever sundered me from thee;
For I permit you ever more
    To borrow your ideas from me.
And thus it is, through weal or woe,
    Our love forevermore endures;
For I permit that you should take
    My views and creeds,
        and make them yours.
And thus, I let you have my way,
    And thus in peace we toil along,
For I am willing to admit
    That I am right,
        and you are wrong.

A PERIODICAL ROMANCE
by Richard L. Evans

(Editor's note: I have included the names of at least 35 magazines, both old and new, in the article below. How many can you find?)

It was mad he knew in these changing times, especially in this old boy's life, to ask a modern woman to join him for a late drink at his apartment.

"True," he had thought to himself, "she thinks I'm very cosmopolitan."

And why wouldn't she think so? Hadn't he lied about making his fortune by crossing national geographic borders and covering sports afield all over the globe?

"What a laugh," he thought again, "my preoccupation with sports illustrated the lack of guide posts in my life." Well, he knew it wouldn't take her long to discover the true story.

She had agreed quickly to go, with what she thought to be just another aging playboy, to his penthouse that Saturday evening, post-haste.

"Why not," she had thought, "don't people still tell me I've the look of a Ms. of just seventeen—a screen star?"
But she knew that a native New Yorker like herself couldn't long feign the glamour associated with the southern living style so much now in vogue. He'd see right through her. It was only a matter of time.

In the end it had been a jet of ebony liquid that had doomed their romance. The spilled espresso had spattered both his shirt and her fashion, then soaked through the magazines on the coffee table. He had never been much of a handyman, so he demanded she get rid of the soggy periodicals for good.

Housekeeping had never been her idea of how a woman's day should be spent but she took them, even though many were no longer being published and left.

WOMAN—A CHEMICAL ANALYSIS

Element: Woman
Symbol: WO = ♀
Discoverer: Adam
Atomic Weight: Accepted as 118,
   but known to vary from 95 to 235.

Occurrence: Copious quantities in all urban areas with slightly lower concentrations in suburban and rural areas. Subject to seasonal fluctuations.

Physical Properties:
1) Surface usually covered with painted film.
2) Boils at nothing, freezes without reason.
3) Melts if given special treatment.
4) Bitter if used incorrectly. Can cause headaches.
5) Found in various states ranging from virgin metal to common ore.
6) Yields to pressure applied to correct points.

Chemical Properties:
1) Has great affinity for gold, silver, platinum and many of the precious stones.
2) Absorbs great quantities of expensive substances.
3) May explode spontaneously if left alone while on a date.
4) Insoluble in liquids, but there is increased activity when saturated in alcohol.
5) Repels cheap material. Neutral to common sense.
6) Most powerful money reducing agent known to man.

Uses:
1) Highly ornamental, especially in sports cars and power boats.
2) Can greatly improve levels of relaxation.
3) Can warm and comfort if given positive circumstances.
4) Can cool things down when it's too hot.

Tests:
1) Pure specimen turns rosy pink when discovered in natural state.
2) Turns green when placed beside a better specimen.

Caution!: Highly dangerous except in experienced hands. Use extreme care when handling.

Illegal to possess more than one.

MAN—A CHEMICAL ANALYSIS

Element: Man
Symbol: MN = ♂
Discoverer: God
Atomic Weight: 180 + or - 100

Occurrence: Haphazard, but may be found in higher concentrations near bars, certain sporting events and crowding around a particularly good specimen of companion element, WO.

Special Properties:
1) Surface often covered with hair, bristly in some areas, soft in others.
2) Boils when inconvenienced, melts if treated like a god.
3) Obnoxious when mixed with alcohol.
4) Tends to fall into very low energy state directly after reaction with WO.
5) Tends to gain considerable mass as specimen ages.
6) When pressure is applied, becomes stiff and unyielding; yields only when subterfuge and/or flattery are applied.
7) Specimens can be found in various states ranging from deeply sensitive to extremely thick.

Chemical Properties:
1) Most forms desire reaction with WO, even when no further reaction is possible. Also usually willing to react with whatever specimen is available.
2) Most powerful, embittering and aggravating agent known to WO.
3) Is repelled by most household appliances and common cleansers.

Uses:
1) Heavy boxes, top shelves.
2) Direct and continuous reaction with TV remote control.
3) "Free" dinners for WO.
4) Methane production. Good specimens are able to produce large quantities on command.

Tests:
1) Pure specimen will rarely reveal purity, while reacted specimens broadcast information on many wavelengths.
2) Solid state at room temperature but easily bent out of shape.

Caution!: In the absence of WO, this element rapidly decomposes and begins to smell.

Oh, death, where is thy sting? It's a lovely day in <u>this</u> neighborhood because an angel has brightened up the place with some balloons. But where is the angel? He's right there in plain sight—can't you see him?

The answer can be found on page 152

GROWING OLD — BUT STAYING YOUNG

What Mother Nature giveth, Father Time taketh away.

YOU KNOW YOU'RE OVER THE HILL WHEN . . .

- You find yourself beginning to like accordion music.
- You're sitting on a park bench and a Boy Scout comes up and helps you cross your legs.
- Your underwear starts creeping up on you . . . and you enjoy it.
- You keep repeating yourself.
- You discover that your measurements are now small, medium and large . . . in that order.
- You light the candles on your birthday cake and a group of campers form a circle and start singing Kumbaya.
- You keep repeating yourself.
- At the airport, they ask to check your bags . . . and you're not carrying any.
- Your insurance company has started sending you their free calendar . . . a month at a time.
- One of the throw pillows on your bed is a hot water bottle.
- You keep repeating yourself.

- It takes you a couple of tries to get over a speed bump.
- You run out of breath . . . walking DOWN a flight of stairs..
- You realize that your worst enemy is gravity.
- At parties you attend, "regularity" is the main topic of conversation.
- Your keep repeating yourself.
- You can plan your own surprise parties.
- You refer to your $2,500 stereo system as "the Hi-Fi."
- You realize that a postage stamp costs more today than a "picture show" did when you were growing up.
- Your childhood toys are now in a museum.
- You sing along with elevator music.
- At the beach you wear black socks with sandals.
- You have a party and the neighbors don't even realize it.

If wrinkles must be written upon our brows, let them not be written upon the heart. The spirit should not grow old.

JAMES A.

GARFIELD

AGE IS A QUALITY OF MIND

Age is a quality of mind.
If you have left your dreams behind,
If hope is cold,
If you no longer look ahead,
If your ambition's fires are dead—
Then you are old.

But if from life you take the best,
And if in life you keep the jest,
If love you hold;
No matter how the years go by,
No matter how the birthdays fly—
You are not old.

ON THE VALUE OF GRAY HAIR
by William Lyon Phelps

It is sad to see so many men and women afraid of growing old. They are in bondage to fear. Many of them, when they find the first gray hair, are alarmed. Now one really ought not to be alarmed when one's hair turns gray; if it turned green or blue, then one ought to see a doctor. But when it turns gray, that simply means there is so much gray matter in the skull there is no longer room for it; it comes out and discolors the hair. Don't be ashamed of your gray hair; wear it proudly, like a flag. You are fortunate, in a world of so many vicissitudes, to have lived long enough to earn it.

RESOLUTIONS WHEN
I COME TO BE OLD

written in 1699 (author unknown)

Not to marry a young woman.

Not to keep young company, unless they desire it.

Not to be peevish, or morose, or suspicious.

Not to scorn present ways, or wits, or fashions,
or men, or war, etc.

Not to be fond of children.

Not to tell the same story over and over to the
same people.

Not to be covetous.

Not to neglect decency or cleanliness, for fear of
falling into nastiness.

Not to be over severe with young people but give
allowances for their youthful follies and
weaknesses.

Not to be influenced by, or give ear to,
knavish, tattling servants, or others.

Not to be too free of advice or trouble any but those
who desire it.

To desire some good friends to inform me which
of these resolutions I break or neglect, and
wherein reform accordingly.

Not to talk much, nor of myself.

Not to boast of my former beauty, or strength, or
favor with ladies, etc.

Not to hearken to flatteries, nor conceive I can be
beloved by a young woman.

Not to be positive or opinionative.

Not too set for observing all these rules, for fear I
should observe none.

AN ANCIENT SPORT

An avid golfer was driving an unfamiliar road one day when he came upon a beautiful golf course he had not seen before. He pulled in and asked at the pro shop if he could play a round for a green's fee. He found he could and was soon standing on the first tee where he was given a choice of three caddies—two young teenagers and an ancient fellow who was at least in his eighties.

He turned to the golf pro standing near by and asked, "Isn't that fellow a little old to be a caddie?"

"Oh no," said the pro, "he's been a caddie here since the course was built 60 years ago. He knows this course as well as he knows the back of his hand."

"Okay," said the golfer, "I'll take him."

The golfer stepped to the tee and drove the ball far down the fairway. Then he turned to the old caddie and asked, "Did you see the ball? I lost it in the sun."

"I sure did," said the caddie. " I saw it off the tee, saw it in the air, saw it land, saw it bounce, saw it roll and saw it stop."

"Great," said the golfer, "where is it?"

"I can't remember."

You will always stay young if you will simply live honestly, sleep sufficiently, eat slowly, work industriously, and lie about your age.

I've finally arrived at that magic age when all the girls want to throw me kisses—but I'm still young enough to prefer that they be delivered in person.

THE ROAD'S LAST TURN
by Henry Van Dyke

Let me but live my life from
*   year to year,*
With forward face and unreluctant
*   soul,*
Not hastening to, nor turning from
*   the goal;*
Nor mourning things that disappear
In the dim past, nor holding back
*   in fear*
From what the future veils;
*   but with a whole*
And happy heart, that pays its toll
To youth and age, and travels on
*   with cheer.*
So let the way wind up the hill
*   or down,*
Through rough or smooth,
*   the journey will be joy,*
Still seeking what I sought when
*   but a boy—*
New friendship, high adventure,
*   and a crown,.*
I shall grow old, but never lose
*   life's zest,*
Because the road's last turn
*   will be the best.*

TRY TO REMEMBER
by Richard L. Evans

I don't know how to break this to you, but aliens will be landing here soon. I can't be sure just what these other beings want with us or this earth, but the mounting evidence of their preparations for invasion should be obvious.

The most compelling bit of proof that aliens have been working to smooth their conquest here is the "dumbing down" of people all over the world. A world full of humans running around like gooney birds should be a pushover for any alien intelligence. You may have noticed that they began the process at the top with our president and the Congress.

I used to think the mental decline among our youth was just the result of a modern liberal attitude toward the upbringing of children; you know the line, "it's all our fault they're as dumb as they are." Well, that's only half of the truth. The aliens have caused us to rear the "I don't know" generation on purpose. And now they're starting to work on me.

Oh, yes! it's happening every day. Just watch me try to remember something—anything.

Scientists tell us (or used to tell us) that an average adult human being should be able to remember seven numbers in a row. That's why our telephone numbers (actually one set of three and one set of four) are set up that way. But can I remember more than one or two telephone numbers any more? Nope.

The aliens have obviously placed some sort of force field around every door jamb in my house. Don't bother to look—you can't see them—but they're there. How do I know? Why else would I forget whatever it was I was going to do or get immediately on entering a new room? There must be things around the door jambs.

The aliens have also installed a "list vaporizer" somewhere in my home. Oh, they're very clever. They knew that I would fight back against their brainwashing campaign by writing down all the things I want to remember, so they've fixed it so that all my lists go "poof" when my back is turned.

I've heard people say that the best thing about senility is that when it happens to you, you won't know it. This is *not true*.

My wife doesn't believe the "aliens are coming" theory. She says I'm just getting older (*better* too, of course—but older). Nevertheless, we should all keep an eye out for the aliens.

"Aliens?" What aliens? I don't remember any aliens.

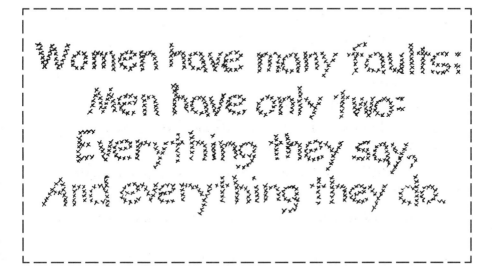

Women have many faults;
Men have only two:
Everything they say,
And everything they do.

The years that a woman subtracts from her age are not lost. They are added to the ages of other women.
COUNTESS DIANE OF POITTERS

SIGNS OF MATURITY
(OR HOW TO KNOW WHEN YOU'RE GROWING OLDER)

1. Almost everything hurts, and what doesn't hurt, doesn't work.
2. The gleam in your eye is from the sun hitting your bifocals.
3. You feel like it's the day after a wild night out on the town, but you haven't been anywhere.
4. All the names in your "little black book" end in M.D.
5. Almost everything is harder to reach, especially your toes.
6. Your children begin to look middle-aged.
7. A dripping faucet never fails to create an uncontrollable urge "down there."
8. You finally know all the answers, but nobody asks you the questions.
9. You look forward to a dull evening.
10. You turn out the lights to save money, not for romance.
11. You sit in a rocking chair but you can't get it going.
12. Your knees will buckle easily but your belt won't.
13. Your back goes out more than you do.
14. The little gray-haired old lady you help across the street is your wife.
15. You have room in every part of the house except the medicine cabinet.
16. You sink your teeth into a nice thick steak and they stay there.
17. You get winded playing chess.

18. You start to compare notes about piles with a neighbor only to discover that *he's* talking about leaves.
19. At least one of your parts won't get up in the morning when you do.
20. You wear a flannel shirt and two sweaters to the Fourth of July picnic.
21. You find yourself saying things like, "rap music is a contradiction in terms."
22. The hair that used to grow on the top of your head now pops out of strange and embarrassing places.

MORE JOYS OF AGING
(adapted)

I have become quite a frivolous old gal. I'm seeing five gentlemen every day. As soon as I awake, Will Power helps me out of bed. When he leaves, I go see John. Then Charley Horse comes along; and when he is here, he takes a lot of my attention.

When he leaves, Arthur Ritis shows up and stays the rest of the day. He doesn't like to stay in one place very long so he takes me from joint to joint.

After such a busy day, I'm really tired and ready to go to bed with Ben Gay.

What a day!

ANTIQUES
by Saydee McLemore

My bed has never been slept in
    By anyone but me;
This chair never was sat in
    Until 1973;
Our dishes came straight from
    The department store,
And never were eaten on
    By anyone else before.
My rugs never saw Persia,
    Or China, or Pakistan,
Nor were trod on by prince
    Or potentate, or holy man.
That lamp came from a sale
    At J.C. Penny's—
Wasn't a wedding present—
    Of Great Aunt Jenny's.
My draperies were a hand-me-down
    With two stains to hide,
My bric-a-brac no objects d'art
    To display with pride.
The picture on the wall
    Came with a case of cereal—
As you can see I'm not
    Burdened by things material;
But welcome to my house,
    Friend and neighbor, kith and kin—
Just open the door and
    Come on in!

THE GOOD OLD DAYS
as retold by Richard L. Evans

For those of us born before 1945, the world has changed a lot. Consider this: we were born before TV, polio vaccine, penicillin, frozen foods, Xerox copies, plastics, contact lenses and "the pill." We were also here before "lite" beer, credit cards, split atoms, ballpoint pens, laser beams, pantyhose, clothes dryers (except the solar-powered kind), dishwashers, air conditioners, electric blankets, jet airplanes and men on the moon.

By today's reckoning, we were sort of peculiar. We got married first, then lived together. Closets in our time were for clothes, not for "coming out of." If someone said he was "gay" it meant he was happy. Our "bunnies" were not big-chested women, but were rabbits—and rabbits were not Volkswagens.

We knew nothing about medicare, baseball strikes, polaroid cameras, shopping malls, frisbees or (thank God) telemarketing.

We thought "fast food" was something you had to eat during Lent. Our idea of outer space was the back row of the Riviera Theater. I can still get light-headed just thinking about it.

We were around before gay rights, house-husbands, computer dating, dual careers, baby-boomers the internet and computer marriages. We came before day care centers, group therapy and nursing homes. We had never heard of FM radios, tape decks, CD disks, rap music, rock and roll, Amway, e-mail, artificial hearts, bioengineering, yogurt, guys with earrings or girls with tattoos. A chip was a little piece of wood; hardware was what you bought in a hardware store (not a "home center"); memory was something you kept to remind you of the past (or lost as you got older); a hard drive was a tough auto trip, and software was nothing at all.

You could "hit the scene" at the 5 & 10 Cent Store. Five cents or a dime would buy a streetcar ride, a phone call, a soda, a postage stamp or a big, juicy (non-reduced-fat) hamburger.

In our day cigarette smoking was fashionable and cheap (20 cents a pack), "grass" was mowed, "coke" was a cold drink, "crack" was a wise remark and "pot" was a cooking utensil.

We were not here before the differences in the sexes but surely before sex changes. We liked the mysteries to be found in the opposite sex and the concept of "unisex" never crossed our minds. We made do with what we had and were the last generation dumb enough to think a girl needed a husband to have a baby.

Is it any wonder we're so addle-brained?

Early to bed, early to rise, and your girl goes out with other guys.

A FATHER'S PROMISE

When I was around 13 and my brother was 10, Father promised to take us to the circus. But at lunch there was a phone call; some urgent business required his attention downtown. My brother and I braced ourselves for the disappointment. Then we heard him say, "No, I won't be down. It will have to wait."

When he came back to the table, Mother smiled and said, "The circus keeps coming back."

"I know," said Father, "but childhood doesn't."

I have enough money to last me the rest of my life—unless I buy something. JACKIE MA-SON

Q: What does an agnostic insomniac with dyslexia do at night?
A: Lies awake wondering whether there really is a dog.

THE BEST PART OF LIFE

We hear a lot these days about what are the "best" years of your life, as if there were a particular age that is the "best." But it isn't how *long* one lives that really matters, only *how* one lives.

The best parts of a man's life are his little unremembered acts of kindness and love. Yes, little things count for much in the world today; the smile of genuine friendliness; the word which gives men renewed courage, the material help which helps someone over a crisis.

It is unfortunate that such ordinary actions do not embody dash and daring and dramatic appeal. People like to do things which excite admiration and stand out as enviable accomplishments. Nearly every person likes to feel he is a potential hero; that if some great challenge were to come, he would meet it unflinchingly. But the occasion for testing one's heroism comes to but few people in a peaceful lifetime.

On the other hand, almost every day it is possible to perform some "little unremembered act of kindness." There are many occasions to help or to encourage another who needs it, occasions to make someone feel a little more hopeful about the world.

Drab and unheroic though this may be, each individual should seize and exploit to the utmost every such opportunity that comes along. That such acts may be the "best" part of man's life is reason enough, but there is an added reason, expressed in these lines:

> *There's a destiny that makes us brothers,*
> *None goes his way alone;*
> *All that we send into the lives of others,*
> *Comes back into our own.*

Ah, the great outdoors! But you'd better watch out if you are hiking in bear country because the bear can sneak up and get you even though you might not see him at first. Can you find the big, bad bear hidden in plain sight?

The answer can be found on page 152

INSPIRATION, GOOD ADVICE AND JUST PLAIN FUN

First life gives you the test—then it gives you the lesson.

YESTERDAY, TODAY
AND TOMORROW

There are two days in every week about which we should not worry, two days which should be kept free from fear and apprehension. One of these days is YESTERDAY with its mistakes and cares, its faults and blunders, its aches and pains. YESTERDAY has passed forever beyond our control. All the money in the world cannot bring back YESTERDAY. We cannot undo a single act we performed; we cannot erase a single word we said. YESTERDAY is gone. The other day we should not worry about is TOMORROW with its possible adversities, its burdens, its large promise and poor performance. TOMORROW is also beyond our immediate control. TOMORROW'S sun will rise, either in splendor or behind a mask of clouds, but it will rise. Until it does, we have no stake in TOMORROW, for it is yet unborn. This leaves only one day—TODAY. Any man can fight the battles of just one day. It is only when you and I add the burdens of those two awful eternities, YESTERDAY and TOMORROW, that we break down. It is not the experience of TODAY that drives men mad—it is the remorse or bitterness for something which happened YESTERDAY and the dread of what TOMORROW may bring. Let us, therefore, live but one day at a time.

**The longest odds in the world
are against getting even.**

HOW TO TELL BAD NEWS

Mr. H: Ha! Steward, how are you, my old boy? How do things go at home?

Steward: Bad enough, your honor; the magpie's dead.

H: Poor Mag! So he's gone. How came he to die?

S: Overeat himself, sir.

H: Did he? A greedy dog; why, what did he get he liked so well?

S: Horseflesh, sir; he died of eating horseflesh.

H: How came he to get so much horseflesh?

S: All your father's horses, sir.

H: What! are they dead, too?

S: Ay, sir; they died of overwork.

H: And why were they over-worked, pray?

S: To carry water, sir.

H: To carry water! And what were they carrying water for?

S: Sure, sir, to put out the fire.

H: Fire! What fire?

S: Oh, sir, your father's house is burned to the ground.

H: My father's house is burned down! And how came it to be set on fire?

S: I think, sir, it must have been the torches.

H: Torches! What torches?

S: At your mother's funeral.

H: My mother, dead!

S: Ay, poor lady! She never looked up, after it.

H: After what?

S: The loss of your father, sir.

H: What! My father gone, too?

S: Yes, poor gentleman! He took to his bed as soon as he heard of it.

H: Heard of what?

S: The bad news, sir, and please your honor.

H: What! More miseries! More bad news.

S: Yes sir; your bank has failed, and your credit is lost, and you are not worth a shilling in the world. I make bold, sir, to wait on you about it, for I thought you would like to hear the news.

Time may be a great healer, but it's a lousy beautician.

It's true that you can't take it with you, but folks ought to remember that how you get it may determine where you go.

One of the great advantages of getting old is that you can sing in the bathroom while you're brushing your teeth.

A COWBOY'S GUIDE TO LIFE

If you find yourself in a hole, the first thing to do is stop diggin'.

Always drink upstream from the herd.

Never miss a good chance to shut up.

Never follow good whiskey with water, unless you're out of good whiskey.

Never smack a man who's chewin' tobacco.

If you get to thinkin' you're a person of some influence . . . try orderin' somebody else's dog around.

There's two theories to arguin' with a woman; neither one works.

Never squat with yer spurs on.

Never kick a fresh cow chip on a hot day.

WHERE DOGS ARE BETTER THAN WIVES

Dogs don't mind it if you leave the toilet seat up.

Dogs think you sing great.

Dogs never need to examine the relationship.

Dogs don't hate their bodies.

Dogs understand that instincts are better than asking directions. (Dogs love long car trips.)

Dogs can appreciate excessive body hair.

Dogs like it when you leave lots of things on the floor.

Dogs don't shop.

Dogs love it when your friends come over.

Dogs don't expect you to call when you're running late.

The later you are, the more excited they are to see you.

Dogs don't care if you use their shampoo.

If a dog is gorgeous, other dogs don't hate it.

THE SYMPTOMS OF
INNER PEACE
by Dr. Jeff Rockwell

1. A tendency to think and act spontaneously rather than from fears based on past experiences.
2. An unmistakable ability to enjoy each moment.
3. A loss of interest in judging self.
4. A loss of interest in judging others.
5. A loss of interest in conflict.
6. A loss of interest in interpreting the actions of others.
7. Frequent, overwhelming episodes of appreciation.
8. Contented feelings of connectedness with others and nature.
9. Frequent attacks of smiling.
10. Increasing susceptibility to love extended by others as well as the uncontrollable urge to extend it.
11. An increasing tendency to let things happen—rather than make them happen.

*Give your troubles to God,
He'll be up all night anyway.*

JUST FOR TODAY
by Sybil F. Partridge

Just for today I will be happy. This assumes what Abraham Lincoln said is true, that "most folks are about as happy as they make up their minds to be." Happiness is from within; it is not a matter of externals.

Just for today I will try to adjust myself to what is and not try to adjust everything to my own desires. I will take my family, my business, and my luck as they come and fit myself to them.

Just for today I will take care of my body. I will exercise it, care for it, nourish it, not abuse it nor neglect it, so that it will be a perfect machine for my bidding.

Just for today I will try to strengthen my mind. I will learn something useful. I will not be a mental loafer. I will read something that requires effort, thought and concentration.

Just for today I will exercise my soul in three ways; I will do somebody a good turn and not get found out. I will do at least two things I don't want to do, as William James suggests, just for exercise.

Just for today I will be agreeable. I will look as well as I can, dress as becomingly as possible, talk low, act courteously, be liberal with praise, criticize not at all, nor find fault with anything and not try to regulate nor improve anyone.

Just for today I will try to live through this day only, not to tackle my whole life's problems at once. I can do things for twelve hours that would appall me if I had to keep them up for a lifetime.

Just for today I will have a program. I will write down what I expect to do every hour. I may not follow it exactly, but I will have it. I will eliminate two pests, hurry and indecision.

Just for today I will have a quiet half hour all by myself and relax. In this half hour, sometimes, I will think of God so as to get a little more perspective into my life.

Just for today I will be unafraid, especially I will not be afraid to be happy, to enjoy what is beautiful, to love and to believe that those I love, love me.

WHAT NOT TO NAME YOUR DOG

Everybody who has a dog calls him "Rover" or "Boy." I call mine, "Sex." He's a great pal but he has caused me a great deal of embarrassment.

When I went to city hall to renew his dog license, I told the clerk I would like a license for Sex. He said, "I'd like one, too!" Then I said, "But this is for a dog." He said he didn't care what she looked like. Then I said, "You don't understand, I've had Sex since I was nine years old." He winked and said, "You must have been quite a kid."

When I got married and went on my honeymoon, I took the dog with me. I told the motel clerk that I wanted a room for my wife and me and a special room for Sex.

He said, "You don't need a special room. As long as you pay your bill, we don't care what you do." I said, "Look, you don't seem to understand; Sex keeps me awake at night." The clerk said, "Funny—I have the same problem."

One day I entered Sex in a contest, but before the competition began, the dog ran away. Another contestant asked me why I was just standing there, looking disappointed. I told him I had planned to have Sex in the contest. He told me I should have sold my own tickets. "But you don't understand," I said, "I had hoped to have Sex on TV." He said, "Now that cable is all over the place it's no big deal anymore."

When my wife and I separated, we went to court to fight for custody of the dog. I said, "Your Honor, I had Sex before I was married." The judge said, "This courtroom isn't a confessional. Stick to the case, please."

Then I told him that after I was married, Sex left me. He said, "Me, too."

Last night Sex ran off again. I spent hours looking around town for him. A cop came over to me and asked, "What are you doing in this alley at four o'clock in the morning?" I told him that I was looking for Sex.

My case comes up Friday.

A CREED TO LIVE BY

Don't undermine your worth by comparing yourself to others. It is because we are different that each of us is special.

Don't set your goals by what other people deem important. Only you know what is best for you.

Don't take for granted the things closest to your heart. Cling to them as you would your life for without them life is meaningless.

Don't let life slip through your fingers by living in the past or for the future. By living your life one day at a time, you live up to your potential all the days of your life.

Don't give up when you still have something left to give—nothing is really over until the moment you stop trying.

Don't be afraid to admit that you are less than perfect. It is this fragile thread that binds us together.

Don't be afraid to encounter risks. It is by taking chances that we learn to be brave. Don't shut love out of your life by saying it's impossible to find. The quickest way to receive love is to give love; the fastest way to lose love is to hold it too tightly; and the best way to keep love is to give it wings.

Don't dismiss your dreams. To be without dreams is to be without hope; to be without hope is to be without purpose.

Don't run through life so fast that you forget not only where you've been but where you're going.

Life is not a race but a journey to be savored every step of the way.

THINGS YOU DON'T WANT TO HEAR
. . . IN SURGERY
from the *International MS Support Foundation*

*Better save that. We'll need it for the autopsy.

*Someone call the janitor; we're gonna need a mop.

*Accept this sacrifice, O Great Lord of Darkness.

*Bo! Bo! Come back with that! Bad dog!

*Wait a minute; if this is his spleen, then what's that?

*Hand me that . . . uh . . . that uh . . . thingie.

*Hey, has anyone ever survived 500ml of this stuff
     before?

*Dang it, there go the lights again.

*Everybody stand back! I lost my contact lens, again.

*Could you stop that thing from beating? It's
     throwing my concentration off.

*What's *this* doing *here*?

*I hate it when they're missing stuff in here.

*That's cool! Now, can you make his leg twitch?

*Well folks, this will be an experiment for all of us.

*Sterile, shmeril. The floor's clean, right?

*Anyone see where I left that scalpel?

*Nurse, did this patient sign the organ donor card?

*She's gonna blow! Everyone take cover.

*What do you mean he wasn't in for a sex change?

**Never give in! Never give in! Never,
never, never. Never—in nothing great
or small, large or petty—never give
in except to convictions of honor and
good sense.** WINSTON CHURCHILL

Natives who beat drums to drive off evil spirits are objects of scorn to smart American motorists who blow horns to break up traffic jams.

MARY ELLEN KELLY

THOMAS JEFFERSON'S TEN RULES FOR THE GOOD LIFE

1. Never put off 'till tomorrow what you can do today.
2. Never trouble another for what you can do yourself.
3. Never spend your money before you have it.
4. Never buy what you do not want because it is cheap; it will be dear to you.
5. Pride costs us more than hunger, thirst, and cold.
6. Never repent of having eaten too little.
7. Nothing is troublesome that we do willingly.
8, Don't let pain cost you the evils which have never happened.
9. Always take things by their smooth handle.
10. When angry, count to ten before you speak; if very angry, count to one hundred.

THE IMPOSSIBLE DREAM
retold by Richard L. Evans

Two men were met by St. Peter as they arrived at the Pearly Gates together. One had been the Pope of the Holy Roman Church for thirty years. The other had been a lawyer.

"Come in, my sons," said St. Peter. Then, putting an arm around each man's shoulder, he ushered them into Heaven.

"Holy Father," said St. Peter to the Pope, "come this way and I'll take you to your eternal home." With that, he led the Pope down a forest path to a ramshackle old shack. Vines had almost covered the dwelling, but gaping holes could still be seen in the roof with the remnants of an outhouse behind. The whole hovel looked as if it could collapse at any moment.

St. Peter then returned to the lawyer and turned him in a different direction. "This," said St. Peter, "will be your home through all eternity." The lawyer could scarcely believe his eyes. There, before him, St. Peter was pointing to a palatial mansion of at least twenty rooms. The lawns and gardens were immaculate. He could also see that parts of the grounds had been devoted to tennis courts, a beautiful swimming pool and an eighteen-hole golf course.

"St. Peter," said the lawyer, "I don't want to seem ungrateful, but I'm very confused. You have given me this wonderful place to live, but the Pope, who served the church all his life, is only given a meager shack. I don't understand.

"It's quite simple," replied St. Peter, "you see, we get lots of Popes up here, but in all the history of mankind on earth, you are the only lawyer we've ever seen."

Editor's note: There are two serious problems with all "lawyer jokes:"

1. Lawyers don't think they're funny.

2. The rest of us don't think they're jokes.

Wisdom consists not so much in knowing what to do in the ultimate — as in knowing what to do next.
HERBERT HOOVER

**To err is human,
but it feels divine.**
MAE WEST

UNNATURAL LAWS
(from all over)

ABEL'S CONSERVATIVE PRINCIPLE: Never do anything for the first time.
CAHN'S AXIOM: When all else fails, read the instructions.
CAPONE'S LAW: You can get much farther with a kind word and a gun than you can with a kind word alone.
FELDSTEIN'S LAW: Never play leap frog with a unicorn.
HUROCK'S LAW: If people don't want to come, nothing will stop them.
LAW OF PREDICTABLE RESULTS: No matter what happens, there is someone who knew it would.
JOHNSON'S LAW OF AUTO REPAIR: Any tool dropped while being used to repair an automobile will roll on the floor to the exact geographic center of the vehicle's undercarriage.

Our prayers are answered not when we are given what we ask but when we are challenged to be what we can be. MORRIS ADLER

126

I WANT TO KNOW . . .
by Oriah Mountain Dreamer
(Indian Elder)

It doesn't interest me what you do for a living. I want to know what you ache for and if you dare to dream of meeting your heart's longing.

It doesn't interest me how old you are. I want to know if you will risk looking like a fool for love, for your dreams, for the adventure of being alive.

It doesn't interest me what planets are squaring your moon. I want to know if you have touched the center of your own sorrow, if you have been opened by life's betrayals or if you have become shriveled and closed from fear of further pain. I want to know if you can sit with pain, mine or your own, without moving to hide it, or fade it, or fix it. I want to know if you can be with joy, mine or your own; if you can dance with wildness and let ecstasy fill you to the tips of your fingers and toes without cautioning us to be careful, be realistic, or to remember the limitations of being a human.

It doesn't interest me if the story you are telling is true. I want to know if you can disappoint another to be true to yourself, if you can bear the accusation of betrayal and not betray your own soul. I want to know if you can be faithful and therefore be trustworthy. I want to know if you can see beauty even when it is not pretty every day, and if you can source your life from its presence. I want to know if you can live with failure, yours or mine, and still stand on the edge of the lake and shout to the silver of the full moon, "Yes!"

It doesn't interest me to know where you live or how much money you have. I want to know if you can get up after a night of grief and despair, weary and bruised to the bone, and do what needs to be done for the children.

It doesn't interest me where or what or with whom you have studied. I want to know what sustains you from the inside when all else falls away. I want to know if you can be alone with yourself and if you truly like the company you keep in the empty moments.

YOU CAN TELL ITS GOING TO BE
A ROTTEN DAY WHEN . . .

. . . you wake up face down on the pavement.

. . . you put your bra on backwards and it fits better that way.

. . . you call Suicide Prevention and they put you on "hold."

. . . you arrive at work only to see a *60 Minutes* news team waiting in your office.

. . . your birthday cake collapses from the weight of the candles.

. . . you decide to put on the clothes you wore home from the party last night and there aren't any.

. . . your twin sister forgets your birthday.

. . . your car horn goes off accidentally and remains stuck as you follow a gang of Hell's Angels on the freeway.

. . . you wake up to discover that your teeth braces are locked together.

. . . you decide to walk all the way to work only to discover when you get there that the back hem of you dress is tucked into the top of your pantyhose.

. . . your income tax refund check bounces.

. . . you decide to chase the fire engine that just passed you to see where it's going and it stops in front of your house.

MY CREED
by Dean Alfange

I do not choose to be a common man. It is my right to be uncommon—if I can. I seek opportunity—not security. I do not wish to be a kept citizen, humbled and dulled by having the state look after me. I want to take the calculated risk; to dream and to build, to fail and to succeed. I refuse to barter incentive for a dole. I prefer the challenges of life to the guaranteed existence; the thrill of fulfillment to the stale calm of Utopia. I will not trade freedom for beneficence nor my dignity for a handout. It is my heritage to stand erect, proud and unafraid; to think for myself, enjoy the benefit of my creations and to face the world boldly and say, this I have done. All this is what it means to be an American.

THE MAN IN THE GLASS

When you get what you want in your
struggle for self,
And the world makes you king for a day,
Just go to a mirror and look at yourself,
And see what that man has to say.

For it isn't your father or mother or wife,
Whose judgement upon you must pass
The fellow whose verdict counts most
in you life,
Is the one staring back from the glass.

Some people may think you are a
straight-shooting chum,
And call you a wonderful guy.
But the man in the glass says you're
only a bum,
If you can't look him straight in the eye.

He's the fellow to please,
never mind all the rest,
For he's with you clear up to the end,
And you've passed your most
dangerous, difficult test,
If the man in the glass is your friend.

You may fool the whole world down
your pathway of years,
And get pats on the back as you pass,
But your final reward will be
heartache and tears,
If you've cheated the man in the glass.

NOTHIN' COULD BE FINER
THAN TO BE IN CAROLINA

I am not a North Carolinian by birth but by choice.

Editor's note: North Carolina is a beautiful state. From the western Great Smoky Mountains, across the piedmont and coastal plain to the outer banks along the Atlantic (where I live), there are few states with such a diversity of scenic wonders. The people, too, are beautiful in their own ways: their warmth; their genuine concern for one another; their grace under pressure; their patience with ill-tempered and rude guests such as—but not limited to— "Yankees." Many North Carolinians are comely in appearance, too.
But not all— which brings us to:

THE PARK RANGER, THE SQUIRREL
AND THE UGLY MAN
retold by Richard L. Evans

A park ranger was driving along a dirt road running through the Croatan National Forest in eastern North Carolina when he spotted an old, beat-up pickup truck parked just off the road. He stopped a few yards behind the truck and was about to get out to investigate the situation when a man stepped out of the woods nearby, approached the truck and threw a large sack into the cargo area. The sack fell open and the ranger could see it was filled with dead squirrels. The other man got in the truck and drove away.

A few days later the ranger saw the same pickup truck parked almost in the same place along the road. Again he stopped and again a man stepped out of the woods with another large sack flung over his back. His curiosity getting the better of him, the ranger got out of his truck and approached the man. As he got closer he could see that the sack was again filled with dead squirrels.

"Excuse me, sir," said the ranger, "I see that you have a large number of squirrels there. Squirrels are not regulated so you can take all you want but I'm curious about how you get so many of them. I see that you don't have a gun."

The other man turned around quickly and the ranger was startled to find himself looking into the ugliest face he had ever seen. The man looked more like a troll than a man. His bulging eyes were set very close together on either side of a large, red-veined nose. His ears stuck out straight from his head and would have rivaled a baby elephant's in size. There were large warts everywhere on his face with a particularly large one on his nose from which grew a long, single hair. When the man smiled, the ranger could see that most of the man's teeth were gone and the few that remained were brown and rotted.

The ugly man said in a friendly manner, "I don't need a gun. When I want to kill a squirrel, I just uglies 'em."

"You 'uglies' 'em'?" said the ranger. "I'm afraid I don't understand."

"Here, I'll show you," replied the ugly man. With that he picked up the sack and motioned for the ranger to follow him back into the forest.

They had only walked a few yards when the ugly man stopped under a large oak tree. On a limb about ten feet above them sat a squirrel. The ugly man looked up at the squirrel and when he was sure the squirrel was looking back at him, he made a terrible grimace which caused his already, incredibly ugly face to become even uglier. The squirrel shuddered at the sight; its eyes rolled back in its head and it fell over backward off the limb, dropping dead at the man's feet.

The ranger was stunned. He said, "I've never seen anything like that! You must be the only person in the world who can do that."

"Nah," said the ugly man as he picked up the dead squirrel, "my wife can do it, too."

The ranger could scarcely believe his ears. "You have a wife?"

"Oh, yeah," replied the ugly man. "I used to take her with me to scare the squirrels, but I can't do that anymore."

"Why not?"

"She tears 'em up too bad."

God brings men into deep waters, not to drown them but to cleanse them.
AUGHEY

WELCOME TO DOWNEAST
NORTH CAROLINA
by Richard L. Evans

Welcome to the real "Downeast." If you live in Memphis or San Diego or Chicago, you may think you are part of the world, but you are not. "The world" to a genuine Carolina Downeaster begins just east of Beaufort, North Carolina (technically at the North River bridge) and runs eastward until it ends at Cedar Island on the Pamlico Sound. That area is "Downeast." Everything else pictured in the world atlas is deemed to be "off."

Downeast isn't just a place; it's a way of looking at life—a philosophical perspective about things that really matter. Things that matter here are God, family, friendships and fishing (also clams, oysters, shrimp and crabs). The people are universally friendly even to people who come from really strange places like Ohio or New Jersey.

People who come to Downeast from "off" are divided into two categories—each with its own label. "Dit-dots" are those from "off" who visit Downeast and then leave. "Ding-batters" are those from "off" who visit Downeast and stay. Most Downeasters prefer Dit-dots.

There is one other named group of Downeasters. "Rubberneckers" get their name from the fact that every bridge over water in N.C. has a "No Fishing From Bridge" sign. You get the idea.

Your life will be rich for others only as it is rich for you.
DAVID McCORD

TWO "OLD" STORIES
retold by Richard L. Evans

It was a bright, beautiful Sunday morning in the small North Carolina town of Beaufort. The townspeople had gathered in the church, and the preacher stood in the pulpit when, suddenly, Satan appeared at the front of the congregation in flame and smoke. Everyone started to scream and to run for the exits in a frantic effort to get away from Evil Incarnate.

Everyone, that is, except one elderly gentleman who sat calmly in his pew watching the Devil. The man didn't' move or seem the least uncomfortable to be in the presence of God's ultimate enemy.

Satan, somewhat mystified by the man's apparent lack of concern for his own safety, approached the man and said, "Don't you know that I am the Prince of Darkness?"

"Yep," said the man.

"Aren't you afraid of me and my terrible powers?" asked Satan.

"Nope," replied the man, "You see I've been married to your sister for 49 years."

Two elderly gentlemen, natives of Swansboro, North Carolina, were out walking one afternoon. As they moved down a path to the White Oak River, they discovered a strange-looking frog in front of them. As they approached, they expected the frog to jump away, but it didn't. One of the men reached down and picked up the frog which immediately said, "(Ribbit), If you'll kiss me, I'll turn into a beautiful, young, (ribbit), girl and I'll be yours for the rest of your (ribbit) life."

The man holding the frog considered the offer for a moment then he gently put the frog into his sweater pocket and continued down the path. "Wait a minute," yelled his old friend, "aren't you going to kiss that frog and turn it into a beautiful young girl who'll be yours for the rest of your life?!"

"Nope," said the man, "at my age, I'd rather have a talking frog."

People say that true friends must always hold hands, but true friends don't need to hold hands because they know the other hand will always be there.

MY BASKETBALL BLUES
by Richard L. Evans

As I write this, it's basketball time again and my neighbors and most of my friends are now temporarily insane —dangerously insane. I, however, am not.

(Ladies, please avert your eyes and mothers, cover your babies' ears.) ***I live in North Carolina and I don't like basketball.*** I also don't particularly care for collard greens (pronounced locally as "coll-yards"). That basketball season and the collard season happen to coincide always gives me the blues.

This admission, I know, will not go down well with many of my acquaintances—some of whom have already asked me why, if I don't like basketball or collards, did I move to North Carolina in the first place? A good question. My answer: who knew? From the frozen north, North Carolina appears to be next to, if not slam in the middle of, Heaven.

But friends, there is a tree that grows in this Garden of Eden each winter. Its leaves are a wrinkled, black-green. In the branches of the tree is a serpent coiled in the shape of a ball— a basketball. Every year North Carolinians eat of the fruit of this tree and fall into the pit. Their minds become clouded with phrases like, "Dump Dook!," "Kill State!" and "To Hell With Carolina!"

I am not entirely alone in my feelings about collard greens and basketball. I once met a fellow—a Tarheel by both birth and comport— who gave me this recipe for collards: "Boil the greens," he said, "in a large, open pot in the kitchen for three days, adding water as necessary. At the end of that time throw the contents of the pot on the ground in the backyard. Then go back into the kitchen and eat whatever you can scrape off the kitchen walls." He said this was the best way to eat collards. In my experience he was right.

There was another fellow (I used to have as many as two friends) who described varsity basketball as a game played by young men and women with severe glandular disorders. These poor souls are required to run back and forth across a hard wooden floor wearing expensive shoes but dressed only in their underwear. The object of this undertaking is to put a round, inflated ball through a steel hoop. The activity required to do this is pretty much the same at each end of the court. This makes for an interesting 30 seconds. I believe my friend overestimated basketball's top interest level by about 25 seconds.

With the end of the cold war, the TV networks and cable systems have had to find something to fill the space formally devoted to the "hate the commies" stuff. What they've found is basketball. Take this challenge: next weekend (any weekend from January through May) use the remote on your TV set to run through every channel you receive. See if you can find a time when there is no basketball being shown or discussed. You won't.

My relative disinterest in basketball would be of no consequence to me or to anyone else except that people temporarily crazed as "basketball manic-depressives" are all around me and they can speak of nothing else. This makes me crazy, too.

As the season progresses and some teams seem headed for more "L's" than "W's," (or what's even worse, an invitation to play in the NIT tournament), the magnitude of conversation between the temporarily insane doesn't wane; it only shifts from what is, to what will be. Recruiting for upcoming seasons becomes the focus of the mania. I know people who can spout the vital statistics (height, weight, scoring average, vertical leaping ability, steals and shot-blocking prowess) of every high school basketball "phenom" within eight states. Those very same people have to search in their pockets or purses to find their own mothers' telephone numbers.

They're crazy and I'm blue.

There are more hogs living in North Carolina than there are people—9.9 million hogs and 7.6 million people.
"Oink!" (Better smile when you say that, partner.)

HOW MANY CAROLINIANS DOES IT TAKE ...
by Richard L. Evans

A few years ago someone told me what he thought to be a good joke. "How many," he said, "(using the name of an ethnic group) does it take to change a light bulb?" When I assured him I didn't know, he gave me the punch line: "Five," he said, "one to hold the bulb and four to turn the ladder." It would have been a good joke, with the image of five people struggling with a ladder and a bulb, had it not been for the obvious slur on the intelligence of the group he had singled out to ridicule. I heard the joke retold several times after that as it made the rounds of clubs and parties.

Then, a peculiar thing started to happen. People began to paraphrase the joke and, in most cases, the joke got better. Here is what happened to the joke when it was applied to the intense rivalry among the three large universities in the Raleigh-Durham-Chapel Hill area:

How many *University of North Carolina* students does it take to change a light bulb?
Two. One to call Daddy and one to go for beer.

How many *North Carolina State* students does it take to change a light bulb?
Only one, but he gets three credit hours *if* he can do it in three tries.

How many *Duke University* students does it take to change a light bulb?
None. *Duke* students are already so bright they don't need light bulbs.

One might guess that the joke was created by one of those "bright" Dukies.

If "ifs" and "buts" were candy and nuts, everyday would be Christmas. "DANDY" DON MEREDITH

SOUTHERN HUMOR

Having lost "The War of Northern Aggression" in the 1860's, the South has taken up another form of warfare: humor. Take this story, for example:

A reporter for the *Raleigh* (North Carolina) *News and Observer* was driving home late one afternoon when he saw a number of people running toward a disturbance on the lawn of a suburban home. As he drew closer, he was horrified to see a large pit bulldog attacking a small child. He stopped his car and ran to the scene. Before he could get there, however, another man had pulled the dog off the child and had managed to subdue the animal only by reluctantly choking it to death.

"What a great story," said the reporter as he got the man's name. "I can see the headline in tomorrow morning's paper: LOCAL MAN SAVES CHILD'S LIFE."

"But I'm not really a local resident," said the man, "I'm just visiting here from my home in Boston."

The next day the newspaper headline read: "YANKEE BASTARD KILLS FAMILY PET."

That, of course, is just a story and there isn't a word of truth in it. But tell it to a Southerner and see how much he enjoys the punch line.

Downeast humor takes many forms. A wonderful example of one of them is the poetic "spoof" of the famous poem, *A Visist from St. Nicholas* found on the opposite page. It was written by this young woman in 1982 for her mother's Sunday School Class at the First Baptist Church in Morehead City, North Carolina.

Connie
McElroy-Bacon

formerly of
Morehead City,
now living in
Raleigh, NC

We "dit dots" and "ding-batters" are sometimes prone to making fun of the patois spoken with such pride by the real "downeasters" whose families have lived here for hundreds of years. But we must admit that it would be hard to find people of such humor and generosity anywhere else. And they can be very "generous" with their humor.

The names used in her poem belong to real people in her mother's Sunday School class. The Munden family owns one of the two funeral homes in this coastal town.

138

'Twas the Night Afore Christmas, Son

by Connie McElroy-Bacon

'Twas the night afore Christmas when all through the house
   — 'neary a thing was stirring, not even Hatie Lee, my spouse.
The waders was a hangin' by the chimney with care
   — in hopes that Santa Claus would fill 'em up thar.
The yungerns was a nestled all snug in thar beds,
   with visions of sweet tatar pies slam filling their heads.
Ma in her sou'wester, and I in my cap,
   had jest settled down to catch us a nap.
When out in da water there rose such a sound
   — I jumped to da window to see if a skiff had run aground.
And don't you think that it weren't a shock
   to see Santa Claus stranded on an oyster rock.
Now that ain't the half of it — there's more.
   The poor ole fellow was awadin' ashore.
I could tell by his looks he weren't none of my kin
   — but, boy let me tell ya — he was mad as a wet hen.
He was a utterin' a word as he went straight to his work,
   'cause he lost one of his boots in da mud
   when he pulled it with a jerk.
Well, he went to da Rice's but thar he got tired,
   trying to get across the sandspurs in their front yard.
He went to the Willis' to give them a lot,
   'till he tripped and fell ona rusty crabpot.
'Bout ready to give up, he went to Zola's down da road
   — and all she got was an ugly oyster toad.
He headed to the Munden's but turned around,
   — figured the way he looked, they'd put him in the ground.
So wet and full of sandspurs, thar he stood;
   he decided he better git while the gittin' was good.
So he swam to the boat ready to leave da island;
   put her in reverse and ran slam into a pilin'.
I heard him holler as he sank outa sight,
"My Lord, Honey, ain't I been momicked this night."

Mr. Homer's Big Hunt

as told by Connie Mason

My Daddy's from a small downeast community called Stacy in North Carolina. Stacy, for its size, is famous for the number of decoy carvers—good carvers from that one community. Not only good carvers, but hunters, also. One of the revered and collectible carvers was my father's boyhood friend, Homer Fulcher. Mr. Homer loved to "kill a duck" just as good as anybody—but goose hunting was a passion.

One night as he lay in his warm, quilt-covered bed, Mr. Homer awoke with a start—sat straight-up in bed from a deep sleep. You know the feeling. You know your ears woke you up to notify your brain that "you need to hear this!!" Mr. Homer strained and heard what he thought was a party going on down the road—a big party—with thousands of people. Only trouble was there weren't a thousand people within a 30 mile radius of Stacy back then. So he got up and opend the window—now the sound made sense—it was a raft of geese on Core Sound—thousands and thousands honking and calling. That calling drew Mr. Homer to his closet like a siren's song where he started grabbing his shotgun with one hand while pulling on his pants with the other. He reached for a box of shotgun shells but they weren't where they were supposed to be. His eyes adjusted to the closet's bare bulb he had flicked on in desperation, and there were his shells scattered along the floor. The kids had been playing with them! No time for thinking about what he was gonna do to those young'uns for gettin' in his closet—he had a mission and dawn was his deadline.

Mr. Homer, armed and armored against the cold, went to the creek and got in his skiff to pole out to his hunting blind. His blind was a stake blind situated three feet above the water, built on four stakes with three sides covered with thatched marsh grass on the outside. Inside, a couple of crude fishboxes served as shelves to hold canned beans and vienna sausages.

Mr. Homer was getting excited now. The eastern sky was showing pink and his eyes were able to make out his objectives' silhouettes. Core Sound was covered with geese. From the sound he knew he was surrounded by geese. Geese to the right—geese to the left—geese in front—and yes, he was goosed from behind—a hunters dream!

Quietly, he reached for the box of shells. But before he could shove a shell in his trusty shotgun, he knew—there was something not right! He had done this thousands of times in the dark and yet something was wrong!

The shells didn't feel right somehow— they, they, they weren't heavy enough. He closed his eyes in a silent prayer of, "Oh, no, this can't be happening to me!" realizing his young'uns had emptied the pellets of shot from all the shells, leaving only the powder. Mr. Homer knew unless he could scare an old goose to death by the sound of a sudden blast that he was "up the blind without a pellet"—a hunter's nightmare.

Now, Downeasters are used to handling bad situations—they aren't prone to panic. And this day, Mr. Homer was bound and determined he was gonna bring geese home—even if he had to jump onto their necks like those calf ropers he'd seen on TV rodeos. But before he could talk himself into jumping in that cold water, his eye was caught by an object on one of those fishbox shelves. He picked it up to examine it in the orange glow of breaking dawn—a pocketknife! A rusted opened—not ever gonna close—tetanus-is-my-middle-name pocketknife.

Well, he says, "I'm gonna use what the Good Lord has provided." So he loaded one of those pelletless shells and then took that old knife and dropped her down the barrell—handle first.

Now the sun was up and as Mr. Homer peeked over the edge of that blind—the most geese mortal man has ever seen at one time—came into view!! And he's got one shot—and he was gonna take it! So, gritting his teeth, he jumped up, aimed into the thickest, densest grouping and let her rip. Baaammm!

That pocketknife flew out of that barrel like a boomerang. Smoke, feathers, panicked birds stampeding flashed over Mr. Homer's head and he fell backwards into the blind. He laid there blinking his eyes, stunned by the sudden silence. He gathered himself up to see if that pocketknife had done its job.

To his delight, he discovered that that knife had decapitated six geese, filleted a dozen mullets and shucked a gallon of salty Core Sound oysters— a hunter's fantasy!

Connie is a native of Carteret County, North Carolina, located near the southernmost of the famed Outer Banks. She is an historian and folklorist with the N.C. Maritime Museum in Beaufort, North Carolina.
She has written numerous stories and recorded many original songs usually centering on life, both now and long ago, in the beautiful Carolina bays, banks, sounds and maritime forests that adorn her native land.

Connie Mason

KIB'S AND THE WHALE CREEK CLUB

by Rodney Kemp

The community store—a Carteret County (NC) tradition—has met the fate of most simple things; about the time you think it will last forever, it's gone. In my growing up in Morehead City, I remember Aspenberg's of Billy View, Ream's of Rabbit Hill, King's of Sunset Shores, Royal's and Willis' on Arendell Street, Springles's of Conch's Point, Yeager's of Camp Glenn, Cherry's and EL Nelson's of downtown Morehead and Kib's of the Promise' Land.

They were all very similar and all very different. For the most part, they featured basic food needs, magazines, tobacco products, kerosene, soft drinks, candy and other treats. They all had personalized charge accounts with the family name in plain view neatly arranged in a Campbell Soup carton or White Owl cigar box. They were different in personality according to who ran them, who hung around them, and what the specialty of the house was.

Aspenberg's featured the pungent, earthy smell of fresh farm produce. Guthrie's had frozen drinks made from real soft drinks. King's had fresh moon pies, cold Pepsi, and the best magazine rack on the East Coast. Royal's had the friendly personalities of Mr. Boyce Royal and his primetime visitor, Coach Gannon Talbert.

The memory of entering the magical world of each and everyone of them with a nickel in tow even today—some forty years later—allows the nostalgic notions to ebb and flow.

Kib's on the corner of 12th. and Evans Street took on the personality of the "banks." It was the hub of the Promise' Land and was owned and operated by the mayor of the Promise' Land, Kilby Guthrie, Jr.

It began as a wooden, rectangular building of "shotgun" architecture if you will. However, it soon developed a distinctive lean to the "eastard" as if to bespeak of the Promise' Land's kinship to the "bankers"who settled in that locale of Cart County. Pictures don't do the lean justice. You had to walk in the door and feel the wall staring at you to understand the full significance of the angle. In Mrs. Helen Baily's geometry classroom at Morehead City High School were displayed models of the common geometric shapes; a square, a rectangle, a triangle, etc. On the model of the trapezoid some enterprising young student had written "Kib's Store." Legend says it was supported by a Ritter Bean can; that's not so! I distinctly remember there were two of them.

Kib's personality was the spirit of the store. My sister was instructed to go inside and purchase a pack of L&M cigarettes for my aunt who was visiting from Pennsylvania. Quickly, Madelyn came back to the car and said, "He wants to know if you want plain or peanut." Cliff Mason walked in one evening and Kib said, "I can tell by the look on your face what you had for dinner." Astonished Cliff listened in amazement as Kib correctly identified the stewed chicken, collards, light rolls, and apple pie that his mom had prepared and put on the table with the welcome invitation, "You crowd, take out and eat."

It never crossed any of the young'uns minds that were victims of Kib's psychic powers to realize he had boxed the order for their mothers.

Being the CEO of a supermarket franchise, Kib was into "marketing." His familiar slogan received national advertising acclaim, "Step right, don't be ashamed, go to Charlie Wallace's and get your purse seine." Kib was the first person to greet the "summer people" who would arrive in the spring. As they unloaded their entourage of children and support people, Kib was right beside them delivering their collards. The "summer people" thrived on such special attention and would have paid almost anything for those collards, which in fact they did.

(continued on next page)

Every spring the Dr. Pepper people would have their logo painted on the outside of that leaning wall. Apparently, the aged, dried wood absorbed the paint because they had to apply several coats to get it right. The smell of that paint was carried for blocks by the breezes and to children on bikes, it sort of announced your entrance into the Promise' Land.

Beside that painted wall was a wooden bench on which sat "the old salts" of the community. I would read the lines in their weathered faces and marvel at the adroitness of their sun-splotched hands and bony fingers as they whittled on their cedar sticks. A chaw of 'backer was everpresent and when one of them spit it usually indicated that the silence was going to be broken by a "short" statement. If a young'un like me wanted to listen to these pearls of wisdom from days gone by, he had to remain perfectly still leaning on the corner of the store and staring down the road as if planning to leave real soon.

Uncle Walter Lewis might say, "Wind's going to the nor'east directly." A few nods and firm whittles would acknowledge the validity of this meteorological forecast.

"Cold toime a-coming," says Capt. Gib Willis following the obligatory spit.

Seconds and minutes would creep by until finally old man Eli Mizelle might say, "Winter of '86, son, talk about cold."

Deep silence would follow as they all would allow their minds to recall the life on Shackleford Banks in a very special, personalized manner. All memories are not to be shared. The best one's are tucked away in the mind's attic to be discovered during those special times when they can be properly dwelled upon and savored for what they represent. "Tain't not nery no one's business what I t'were a-thinking, son."

Those men—The Whale Creek Club—were treasures I appreciated then but even more now. They represented the genuine independence of the "bankers'" life-style. They were the one's who had experienced the culture shock of having moved

144

from the banks to "civilization." They longed to go back. The concluding line of Gretchen Guthrie's poem, "The Old Man and the Child" says:

Out there, oh no, o'er there on Shackleford Banks
Are the wonder years of long ago.

It was always said that Kib's store was condemned and would be torn down when he died. This in fact must have been true because a vacant lot represents its position now. I don't remember when it was razed. I don't want to know. I don't like change. Oh, I appreciate the wide aisles of the Food Lion, Winn-Dixie, or the A&P and the convenience of loading up your own cart. However, there was something mystical to a child the way Kib or any of the others who operated these community stores would reach high on the shelf with their hooked stick, snare a box of Quaker Oats, and catch it as it tumbled down. But, I'll just tuck that memory away and someday I may be addressed as "old pa" and can share it in the manner of the Whale Creek Club.

Rodney Kemp

Born in Knoxville, Tennessee, Rodney moved with his family to Morehead City, North Carolina at age three.

After gaining his degree from Texas Tech University, he returned to Morehead City in 1969 and began a 14-year teaching career.

Rodney entered the insurance business in 1983 but continues to use his love of history, teaching about his home county using humorous stories as illustrations. He speaks, performs, preaches or teaches about 150 times a year—a schedule he has maintained for the last nine years. And, as if that weren't enough, he appears regularly on a local television sports show called, "Bleacher Seats."

Rodney is proud to be known as a "Fishhouse Liar" (a title of respect earned only by those who have the greatest of storytelling abilities along with a healthy disregard for the truth).

THREE DOWNEAST DUCK HUNTING STORIES
by Rodney Kemp

BULLET GOES HUNTING

Cap'n Monroe of Cedar Island was known for his skills as a duck hunter and his expertise as a hunting guide. He also took great pride in his ability to train dogs to help in these endeavors.

Normally extremely gregarious, there was a spell there when he refused to let anyone go hunting with him except for his dog, "Bullet." He also refused to allow Bullet to go with any hunting parties he was guiding.

One day Mr. J.W. Jackson, one of the principal owners of the "Hog Island Hunting Club," demanded that he bring Bullet along with just the two of them for a hunt. Now the Hog Island Hunting Club was Cap'n Monroe's main source of income and he felt obliged to comply although with some strange apprehension.

They were in the blind right near Harbor Island when a lone duck appeared on the eastern horizon. Mr. Jackson aimed and dropped that duck with one shot. Mr. Jackson motioned for Monroe to send Bullet for the kill and, somewhat reluctantly, he gave the command.

Bullet "tip-toed" across the top of the water, picked the duck up and "tip-toed" back ever so gently. Neither gentleman spoke.

Another lone duck appeared; Mr. Jackson shot him successfully, and once again Bullet "tip-toed" across the water to fetch him back.

Mr. Jackson said, "I didn't say anything the first time, but when I saw it again, I've got to comment about what that dog is doing."

"Don't say anything," Cap'n Monroe said apologetically, "I'm embarrassed enough about the fact that I have never been able to teach that dog to swim."

DUKE DONE IT!

Bone-chilling cold assisted by a brisk wind from the nor'east wrapped Cedar Island in winter as the two men and their dogs headed for Hog Island before daylight for their limit of ducks.

Old Duke, Howard Douglas's faithful black lab, trembled with excitement at the anticipation of shotgun blasts and flying feathers.

Lester Gray broke the silence by saying "Old Trooper here is probably the best duck dog in these parts."

"He's the second best in this boat," replied Howard, "and five bucks says I can prove it."

The bet was on and Duke was given first chance.

When the boat reached the landing, Duke leaped out of the boat and headed up the shore. Lester Gray laughed at such undisciplined behavior and said this would be the easiest five bucks he'd ever made.

Directly, Duke came speeding back towards the blind, dropped on his belly and held up one paw.

"What's he doing?" asked Lester Gray. "He's telling us one duck is approaching and we'd better be ready."

Bang! went the shot from Howard Douglas's gun and Duke, after proudly retrieving the kill, headed back up the shore.

Shortly, here came Duke. Again, he dropped on his belly but this time perked up both ears.

"There's two of 'em coming and they're flying low." Bang! Bang! the guns fired simultaneously and both ducks landed on the water so even Trooper, in a state of shock, had something to do. Gone again was Duke.

This time he came running back with a stick in his mouth while shaking his head wildly.

Lester Gray couldn't stand it any longer and said, "Okay Howard, what in the hell does that mean?"

"It means you owe me five bucks and there are more ducks coming than you can shake a stick at."

written by Rodney Kemp

as told to him by David Yeomans

CAP'N FRED GOES DUCK HUNTING
by Rodney Kemp

Cap'n Fred and Howard Douglas went duck hunting down at Cedar Island one cold morning and Howard took along a thermos bottle full of coffee while Fred had a bottle of Old Typesetter (one slug and you're through). Both imbibed freely of their chosen beverages through the early hours and finally, a lone duck appeared heading toward the blind.

Howard Douglas raised his gun first, took aim and fired. The duck kept on going. Cap'n Fred pointed his gun at the duck and brought it down with the first shot.

"That's pretty good shooting," said Howard. "Nothin' to it," said Cap'n Fred. "When a flock like that comes over, you're bound to kill one of them.

CAP'N FRED GETS MARRIED
by Rodney Kemp

Cap'n Fred married Miss Hilda in May of 1939. In honor of this occasion, Uncle "Leigh" offered Fred the use of his 1936 Ford Roadster for the honeymoon trip. In Fred's mind, the anticipation of driving that car rivaled that of the wedding itself.

With the nuptials completed, Fred and his new bride were driving away from Cedar Island toward their honeymoon rendezvous. Hilda finally broke the silence by saying, "Fred, I am so happy. Where are we going to spend our honeymoon?"

"Beaufort," Fred replied.

Overcome by the ecstasy of driving Uncle "Leigh's" car with his beautiful mate beside him, Fred slowly placed his arm around Hilda's shoulder.

She said, "Now that we're married, you can go much further than that, Fred."

And he did. He drove all the way to New Bern.

"SOMETIMES IT'S BETTER TO BE
DEAD THAN ALIVE"
by Rodney Kemp

Cap'n Fred often used the phrase, "Sometimes it's better to be dead than alive." And he had good reason for making this statement.

Along with lying, Cap'n Fred also enjoyed so very much the "fruits of the vine;" that is to say he drank hard liquor every chance he got.

It seems he was so serious about his drinking that he built and operated his own "whiskey still" in the woods behind his house.

Miss Hilda, Cap'n Fred's God-fearing, bible-thumping, temperance-believing wife discovered the illegal still, destroyed it and told Cap'n Fred if he ever again made his own spirits, she would kill him.

Riding back from Beaufort late one Saturday evening with his drinking buddy steering the car by squinting through one eye in the traditional Down East method of "keeping her between the ditches," the car suddenly skidded sideways, righted itself and went head first into the canal on the left side of the road. Cap'n Fred was slung out the passenger side window onto the ditch bank. A passerby noted that there was no life visible in Cap'n Fred and they hurried to relay the tragic news to Miss Hilda.

Miss Hilda grabbed her hat, shawl and pocketbook and headed for the accident scene. She never went anywhere without her quilted pocketbook which, people swear, weighed upwards to eight pounds loaded.

She held Cap'n Fred's head in her lap and explained how much she loved him. She said if he would just come back to life, she would never again chastise him for his drinking or lack of meaningful employment. She said she was sorry for all the hateful things she ever said to him and asked his forgiveness for the beatings she administered to him with her lethal pocketbook. As she broke into sobs, she said, "Please come back my dear Fred and everything will be different."

At that, one of Cap'n Fred's eyes opened and he whispered, "Let me have my whiskey still back and I believe we've got a deal."

The startled Miss Hilda began to lambast away at Cap'n Fred's head with that pocketbook provoking him to say as he struggled to survive, "Boys, I was a way lot better off dead than alive."

We North Carolinians will be mighty proud of our state roads (someday).

Before you tackle the application form at the right, you might want to take a little primer on one of North Carolina's major past-times (right behind basketball and "pig picking") namely, road working.*

KEY TO CORRECT ROAD WORKING SYMBOLS:

(A) **State mineral**   (B) **State statue**   (C) **State flower**

(D) **Sate animal**   (E) **State flag**   (F) **State motto**

(G) **State joke**   (H) **State joke (politically correct)**

* This might lead one to conclude that this is the reason North Carolina is known as the "Tarheel State." This is not true.

APPLICATION TO LIVE IN NORTH CAROLINA

FIRST NAME_____ LAST NAME (if known) _____ NICKNAME _____ CB HANDLE _____
RFD ADDRESS _____
DADDY (if unknown, list possible suspects)_____
MAMA'S NAME _____ MAIDEN NAME (if different) _____
SPOUSE _____ FORMER RELATIONSHIP (check only one) ☐ BROTHER ☐ SISTER
☐ AUNT ☐ COUSIN ☐ UNCLE

NECK SHADE (check only one): ☐ LIGHT RED ☐ MEDIUM RED ☐ DARK RED ☐ NO NECK

MAKE/MODEL OF PICKUP TRUCK _____ BRAND OF LIFT KIT INSTALLED _____
NUMBER OF EMPTY BEER CANS ON FLOOR OF TRUCK _____ NUMBER OF RIFLES IN GUN RACK _____
OPTIONAL EQUIPMENT INSTALLED (check all that apply) ☐ GUN RACK ☐ 8-TRACK ☐ 4-WHEEL DRIVE
☐ RUNNING BOARDS ☐ ROLL BAR ☐ DOG CAGE ☐ MUD FLAPS ☐ FUZZ BUSTER ☐ WINCH
☐ LOAD OF WOOD ☐ CAMPER SHELL ☐ CONFEDERATE FLAG ☐ HIJACK SHOCKS
☐ DUAL CB ANTENNA ☐ AIR HORNS ☐ RACOON TAIL ☐ LINKED-CHAIN LICENSE PLATE HOLDER
BUMPER STICKERS (check all that apply):
☐ "EAT MORE POSSUM" ☐ "FREE MUSTACHE RIDES" ☐ "HONK IF YOU LOVE JESUS"
☐ "SHIT HAPPENS" ☐ "WAVE IF YOU'RE HORNEY" ☐ "REDMAN CHEWING TOBACCO"

CULTURAL RECOGNITION TEST (define the following - must get at least 12 right):
1. GRITS _____ 8. GOOBERS _____
2. SIDEMEAT _____ 9. CHITLINS _____
3. BRUNSWICK STEW _____ 10. MOON PIE _____
4. REDEYE GRAVY _____ 11. JAIL BAIT _____
5. FATBACK _____ 12. TATER _____
6. PORK RINDS _____ 13. STUMP BROKE _____
7. FISH MUDDLE _____ 14. TARHEEL _____

HOBBIES (check all that apply): ☐ COW TIPPIN' ☐ COON HUNTIN' ☐ DRANKIN' ☐ PITCHIN' SHOES
☐ DEER SPOTIN' ☐ COW CHIP PITCHIN' ☐ SPITTIN' BACK ☐ PICKIN' & GRININ'

FAVORITE VOCALISTS (check all that apply): ☐ SLIM WHITMAN ☐ CONWAY TWITY ☐ WILLIE NELSON
☐ JOHNNY CASH ☐ LORETTA LYNN ☐ HANK WILLIAMS ☐ BOXCAR WILLIE ☐ ROGER WHITAKER
☐ RANDY TRAVIS ☐ ELVIS ☐ GEORGE JONES ☐ REBA MCINTIRE ☐ SHANIA TWAIN

CROPS RAISED: ☐ CORN ☐ PEANUTS ☐ TOBACCO ☐ COLLARDS ☐ RUG RATS

FAVORITE BREAKFAST: ☐ PEPSI & NABS ☐ TANG ☐ BUDWEISER ☐ REDMAN

WEAPONS OWNED: ☐ DEER RIFLE ☐ SHOTGUN ☐ CHAIN SAW ☐ BALL BAT ☐ TIRE IRON ☐ 2 X 4
☐ PIT BULL ☐ PICK HANDLE ☐ CARPENTER'S LEVEL

NUMBER OF HOUND DOGS OWNED: BLUE TICK _____ BLACK & TAN _____ BLOOD _____
CAP EMBLEM: ☐ JOHN DEERE ☐ VFW ☐ VIGORO ☐ CAT ☐ NRA ☐ 84 LUMBER ☐ CAMELS
CURRENT NUMBER OF WEEKS UNEMPLOYED:_____ NUMBER OF WELFARE CHECKS RECEIVED: _____
NUMBER OF DEPENDENTS: (legal)_____ (claimed) _____
LENGTH OF LEGS: (right)_____ (left)_____
MEMBERSHIPS (check all that apply): ☐ KKK ☐ NRA ☐ VFW ☐ PTL ☐ MINUTEMEN

Please supply the follow information:
DOES YOUR TRUCK HAVE ANY PARTS PAINTED WITH RED PRIMER (OFFICIAL STATE COLOR)? _____
HOW MANY CARS DO YOU HAVE SITTING ON BLOCKS IN YOUR FRONT YARD? _____
HOW MANY KITCHEN APPLIANCES DO YOU KEEP ON YOUR FRONT PORCH? _____
WHEN WAS YOUR LAST ELVIS SIGHTING?_____ WHERE?_____
DOES YOUR WIFE WEIGH: ☐ AS MUCH AS YOUR PICKUP TRUCK? ☐ MORE THAN YOUR PICKUP TRUCK?
HAVE YOU EVER BEEN SOBER FOR AN ENTIRE WEEKEND?_____ IF SO, WHY?_____
CAN YOU SIGN YOUR OWN NAME AND GET IT RIGHT? ☐ ALWAYS ☐ SOMETIMES ☐ SELDOM

DO NOT WRITE BELOW THIS LINE

- -
FOR OFFICAL USE ONLY

APPLICATION IS **ACCEPTED**
  REASON(S)
  ☐ GOOD OLD BOY
  ☐ MY COUSIN
  ☐ REFUSES TO VOTE
  ☐ KNOWS RICHARD PETTY

APPLICATION IS **REJECTED**
  REASON(S)
  ☐ LACES ON BOTH SHOES TIED
  ☐ WEARS POLO SHIRT
  ☐ HAS OWN TEETH
  ☐ CAN'T SPIT

ACKNOWLEDEGMENTS

I gratefully acknowledge the following companies and individuals who have helped to make this book possible:

The Baltimore Sun, from the book, *Motherhood is a Contact Sport* by Susan Reimer; *DePauw* (Universtiy) *Magazine*, Mike Lillich, editor and Geofrey Garrett; Houghton Mifflin; Rodney Kemp; Connie Mason; Connie McElroy-Bacon; Saydee McLemore; *Pulpit Helps*, Ted Kyle, managing editor; "We Bereaved," copyright 1929 by Leslie Fulenwider, Inc. from THE OPEN DOOR by Helen Keller. Used by permission of Doubleday, a division of Random House, Inc.; "I Believe," from MIDSTREAM by Helen Keller. Copyright 1929 by Helen Keller and The Crowell Publishing Company. Used by permission of Doubleday, a division of Random House, Inc.

I should also like to acknowledge many others (in no particular order) who have gone out of their way to help me with publications over the years: Chris Couch, Greta and Henry Boshamer, Debbie and Markey Burroughs, Dennis Evans, Mary Kirk, Terrie and Mike Street, David Ingalls, Carolyn Lyle Evans, Laura Evans-Blake, Lyle Evans, Ken Fish, Rene Minshew, Tim Havlicek, Dana Wade, Jeanne and John Mays, David Cloud, Donnie Jones, William Faulkner, Bernie Whalley, William C. Kramer, Melanie S. Harper, Jim Walker, Mary Alford, Glenn Thatcher, John Collison and Mike Heath.

Answers to the hidden illustrations

page 6

page 46

page 70

page 86

page 100

page 114